# Secrets of
# **SUCCESSFULL**
# **Spa Owners**

*Jeremy Baker*

DISCLAIMER AND/OR LEGAL NOTICES:

The information presented herein represents the view of the author as of the date of publication. Because of the rate with which conditions change, the author reserves the right to alter and update his opinion based on the new conditions. The report is for informational purposes only. While every attempt has been made to verify the information provided in this report, neither the author nor his affiliates/partners assume any responsibility for errors, inaccuracies or omissions. Any slights of people or organizations are unintentional. If advice concerning legal or related matters is needed, the services of a fully qualified professional should be sought. This report is not   intended for use as a source of legal or accounting advice. You should be aware of any laws which govern business transactions or other business practices in your country and state. Any reference to any person or business whether living or dead is purely coincidental.

# Table of
# CONTENTS

# WHO AM I?

I help Day Spas and Med Spas reach their growth potential and dominate their markets by implementing proven marketing systems. My job is to be an expert in marketing, and specifically local marketing that leverages technology to achieve maximum results, so that my clients can focus on what they do best; **serve their clients.**

The goal of this book is to not only teach the marketing systems that are working now, but also what other successful industry professionals are doing to ensure their success. I've got a lot to share with you about how you can dominate your market and take your income to entirely new levels, but of course we have limited time together, so I am going to do my best to give you the high points over the course of this book and then the interviews will follow.

I look forward to sharing what's working, in getting more customers and **better quality** spa customers today.

Let me begin by first thanking all of those industry professionals that contributed to this book. This book would not be the same without you! When I talk with spa owners, 3 critical marketing issues typically come up; How best to reach as many consumers as possible that would fit an ideal client profile for their services, How those consumers are making purchasing decisions about spa services & aesthetic treatments today, and How to convert them into loyal clients for life. The answers to these questions are what follows.

My purpose is to begin what to many, may be a dramatic change in beliefs about Spa marketing. What's possible, what works, and how to grow your business by leveraging digital marketing strategies.

The magnitude of information lodged at consumers on a daily basis causes them to guard their attention closely. Grabbing your ideal client's attention requires producing content that evokes emotion, solves problems, and addresses questions and concerns better than that of your competitors. That's a tall order.

The goal of an effective new client acquisition marketing campaign is targeting your ideal client and getting their attention. You want consumers who respond to your marketing strategies and become loyal customers for life; clients who come back and pay full price for more and bring in thousands of dollars in revenue year after year.

First, I want you to know that this is POSSIBLE. This is the first step of the mind-shift, away from a daily deal based marketing model, which I find so many Spa & Salon owners are stuck in.

*So how do we accomplish this?*

The consumer journey has changed in the last few years and the type of consumer you want to attract is not hunting for deals on coupon sites but rather, researching who would be the BEST Spa or Med spa to treat them, and who they know, like and can trust.

What I'm about to show you, can ignite growth at your business well beyond the levels you've likely achieved in the past.

There are 4 critical marketing systems that need to be implemented to achieve growth. 90% of the clients I have worked with over the years are missing AT LEAST two out of the four of these critical, proven marketing systems. While the clients who are leveraging all four? They're growing.

Unless your situation is completely out of the ordinary (which is possible but unlikely), **there is a really big opportunity to accelerate the growth of your business by leveraging the power of digital media.**

In Fact, these four elements are the foundational building blocks that every successful business must optimize, in order to achieve the growth they're looking for. But again, my experience tells me that most Spas are not taking complete (or efficient) advantage of each of the four pieces.

I am talking about sustainable and responsible growth—the kind that complements your ethical standards and supports your long-term vision for your business.

The continued development and distribution of technology has radically changed the way consumers are buying—how they hear about products and services; how they research them, and how they make a final purchase decision. There are three main drivers of this change that are impacting your business. You need to be aware of them. Let's run through each major driver.

▼

# SEARCH

First, let's take a look at the numbers. According to recent poll data from the Pew Internet and American Life Project, 92% of adult Internet users in the U.S. use a search engine (e.g. Google, Bing) to find information online—with the majority of this group performing keyword searches on a regular basis. When you look at educated and affluent individuals, search engine use climbs to as high as 98 percent.

These statistics simply underline what you and I already know:

## SEARCH IS KING.

Everyone who has access to the Internet uses a search engine to find relevant and useful information, and according to Google's own data, 97% of consumers search for local businesses online.

## GOT VISIBILITY?

The upshot of these facts is clear:

If you want visibility for your business, you need visibility in the search engines, particularly Google.

Search isn't just king; it's a kingmaker too. High visibility in Google can mean more website traffic, more customers and referrals, more sales activity, thereby leading to an increase in profit for your business. For Spas in hyper-competitive markets, search-engine visibility can be the difference between being an unknown also-ran and being the Top Dog.

## THE GOOD, THE BAD AND THE UGLY: THERE FOR ALL TO SEE.

But visibility is a double-edged sword. Customer reviews of your business are visible too. What if some of these reviews are negative? What if they're scathing?

Well, the bad news is they can haunt your business for years and have a crushing impact on your bottom line. On the flip side, good reviews can fuel positive word of mouth and generate referral traffic like you've never seen!

We've all heard enough hype about social media to last a lifetime (or two). But there's a good reason, because there's actually something to the hype. The social web has truly been a game changer.

## SUDDENLY THE NORM.

The rapid rise of social media is astonishing. Just think: Facebook grew from a curiosity in a Harvard dormitory to a global force with over 1,000,000,000 users ... in less than a decade. Facebook seems like old news now—a presence in our lives that we take for granted—but it's worth remembering how recently this shift has taken place.

People aren't just ON social networks. They're GLUED to them. The average U.S. Facebook user spends 7 hours and 46 minutes on the site each month. That's a full 15.5 minutes the average American spends on Facebook every single day! The upshot of all of these numbers is pretty straightforward, but I'll spell it out just in case:

## YOUR CUSTOMERS ARE ON FACEBOOK & INSTAGRAM.

Not only are they on social networks but they spend a LOT of time there. They're also sharing, tweeting, liking, pinning, friending, starring, following, fanning, posting, hash tagging, uploading, retweeting ... you name it! So if you want to reach them, capture their attention and make a pitch for your services before your competitors do ... you've got to at least meet them halfway.

Keep in mind; however, it does no good to have a Facebook or Instagram account if you don't post on it regularly. We recommend daily postings.

It is important to understand; however, unless you have thousands of fans on your business Facebook page, your messages are not getting noticed. The "organic" reach of your posts is at about 5-10% of your page Fans to start with, so the posts need to be promoted to a targeted group of your ideal clients for maximum engagement.

Make sure you regularly post helpful content or links to your site where you have interesting content ready for your customers, or audience, to enjoy.

We recommend using a social media management platform to streamline & simplify social media management.

A quick Google search will show the many options available on the market, ranging from free to $1,000 a month. The key features to look for on any platform are:

- *The ability to easily find relevant and engaging content, & create high impact image posts with ease.*

- *Schedule the content to Post to all your social networks at once.*

- *The ability to measure best performing content / hashtags, find optimal times of day to post & easily reschedule the most successful content.*

## SHARING EXPERIENCES ... AND FRUSTRATIONS

People are taking to the web to share their experiences with brands, and what they're sharing with their friends and family members isn't always flattering...

According to a study from the Society for Communications Research, 59% of U.S. consumers are using social media to vent about customer care frustrations. This isn't just happening on Facebook, but on sites like Angie's List, Yelp, Google and others.

More and more businesses are beginning to realize that, while they can't always control what people say online, they can (and should) monitor and contribute to the conversation in an effort to influence the overall tenor.

They're realizing that having a proactive online presence that's focused on adding value to the customer experience is the surest way to grow and preserve their brand's reputation—and protect themselves from the stray musings of a few unhappy souls.

## KEEPING PACE WITH BUYER EXPECTATIONS.

Another big reason to get actively involved in social media is that you have to do it to stay relevant. Your buyers expect it, and if you fall short of their expectations, they'll be more likely to spend their money with the Spa down the street.

Even way back in 2008, a Cone Business study on social media found that 93% of customers expected companies to have a presence on social channels, and 85% expected companies to interact with them on those social channels on a daily basis. That figure has only grown as the social media era has matured. You can either join the conversation or let your competitors do all the talking. It's up to you!

It's almost impossible to overestimate the impact of the mobile computing revolution. In fact, the proliferation of cell phones, smart phones, e-readers and tablet PCs might be one of the most underestimated and under-hyped shifts in business today. Today, 87% of Americans have mobile phones. It's their No.1 most-used technology device, with 73% their desktop PC.

It's clear that the future of the web is tied to smartphones, tablets and other mobile devices. People who visit your website will most likely do so from a small-screened device, instead of a hulking desktop or laptop.

What does that mean to you, being the local Spa owner? It means that if you want an effective web presence that supports your business goals, you need to have a website that supports a multitude of platforms, specifically the smart phone.

In fact, a study from Google found that 6 in 10 mobile users will leave a website if it's not optimized for small screens. If your business' site looks cramped, cluttered, or illegible when viewed on a tablet or smart phone, you run the very real risk of turning away your most valuable asset; your customers. Making matters even worse, Google started penalizing non-mobile friendly websites back in April of 2015, so if you're not mobile-friendly yet, your website's ranking on search results pages has probably dropped – meaning your businesses visibility and lead generation has also dropped.

If your organization doesn't already have a mobile responsive web design, you better get one quickly.

**Let's put this into perspective ...**

People still worry about losing their jobs. Many homeowners owe more on their mortgage loans than what their homes are worth. Credit-card debt continues to weigh down U.S. households. As a business owner, you don't want to give them any more reasons not to spend money at your Spa. Furthermore, you don't want to add any additional friction to the process of calling to book an appointment or booking from your website.

**A streamlined website for mobile is a must-have.** Particularly, when you consider that people with smartphones are still turning to search engines to look for information.

## SEARCH TO PURCHASE

What's more, studies show that when people use their smart phones to search for information, they're more apt to take immediate action. They search from where they are and go immediately to what they find.

*THE IMPORTANT THING NOW IS TO ASK THE HARD QUESTIONS AND SEEK OUT THE ANSWERS—EVEN IF THEY SHAKE THINGS UP A BIT:*

▼

- *How do these changes impact the way consumers interact with my business?*

- *How do these changes impact the growth of my business?*

- *How do these changes impact the way I approach the marketing of my Spa?*

Given all of these changes we've discussed
**search, social and mobile**

you might be worried that you are going to have to make drastic, revolutionary changes in your business. That's not necessarily the case.

Our experience shows that there are four key marketing systems that need to be optimized, in order to maximize growth in today's wired, always-on and hyper-competitive marketplace.

Before we get into the marketing systems that need to be optimized, I want to begin with an example of what's **NOT** working.

# DAILY DEALS.

Many I talk to in this industry, share a similar frustration with daily deal sites. They feel like they are forced to discount their services by 50% or more to get new clients in the door. In most cases, this is bad business and is not a long-term strategy for maximizing revenue from your services.

For example:

If you are offering a $1000 (full retail) laser hair removal deal for $100, Groupon will keep $50 of that. So that leaves you with $50 which does not even get paid back to you in full, right away. Now, let's say that 200 people purchase that deal from Groupon. The business will still need to pay for the number of staff needed to serve the huge increase in customer flow, the cost of supplies, use of equipment, etc. At the end of the day, you may be left with a profit of just $10 of a regularly priced $1000 service. If the client doesn't return, the spa is only not making money, they are also losing it. Additionally, **they are losing opportunities to generate full-priced retail services in that same time slot.** It's no wonder Daily Deal sites have caused so many businesses to close their doors or jump ship because they can't continue to offer their services at such ridiculously low rates. It's a vicious cycle.

Let's say within in a span of 48 hours, you sold 200 of these deals. It's great for business right? Wrong. Not only are you making 5%-10% of your original profit, but how are you going to accommodate 200 new clients? Phones are ringing off the hook, the reception area is packed with new clients and staff needs to put in extra hours, to be able to fit everyone in. It's impossible to keep up so you have to cut corners somewhere—and that somewhere is in the quality of service. This happens all the time!

Appointment times are delayed for months because of the large number of new deal clients. Treatments are done quickly and carelessly, causing more pain to the client. Botox is diluted way more than it should be and lasts for 2 weeks instead of 4 months. Massages are cut short and rushed... etc.

**The point here is that, no matter what your specific profit or loss would be on deals offered, service levels are often not the same as they are with full priced clients. When the quality of service drops, you are left with an unhappy new client, and I don't know anyone who would want 200 new unhappy clients. Because, guess where daily deal customers go when they are not happy? To online review sites such as yelp and Google where their bad reviews will trash your business and leave you with a reputation that will be hard to reverse. The vast majority of negative reviews I come across are those from daily deals.**

A quick Google search will turn up hundreds of pages that are filled with negative experiences business owners have had with daily deal sites.

The unfortunate reality is that, unlike the loyal long-term clients you want for your spa, daily deal customers have no loyalty to you, whatsoever. Not only are they more critical than your usual clients, they are also more likely to complain. Research has shown that less than 10% of daily deal customers ever return for a second visit. They are not the customers that will support your business through thick and thin and that will spread their positive experience with their friends.

The race to the bottom never ends. Discounting makes you appear desperate. Buyers sense that, and this is why they have no loyalty to you when they make decisions solely based on the size of the discount. This takes you out of control. **I want to put you back in control.**

There are times however, when running discount campaigns for lead generation and customer acquisition makes sense.

We have run many successful viral Facebook campaigns to generate new appointments from new clients, using discount offers. The advantage of using the power of social media to run your own promotions is that, you now have all the contact info of your leads, enabling you to create a follow-up system for repeat business from them. There needs to be a follow-up system in place to get them back!

*How do you get deal hunting customers back?*
*How can you up-sell them?*

One of the tools we use for our clients is text message marketing. We get discount hunting consumers back by asking them to redeem their discount with their contact info, first name, a mobile number and birthday. We are then able to send them a mobile coupon with a nice graphic and a special offer to get them back in the door, without having to discount 50%.

We use the mobile numbers of the deal seekers to attract the type of client we want from this group. The offer is sent via text with a small discount for use at a time that is convenient for the Spa, based on openings in the schedule that need to be filled within a few hours' notice.

# THE 4
# **KEY ELEMENTS**
## FOR GROWTH

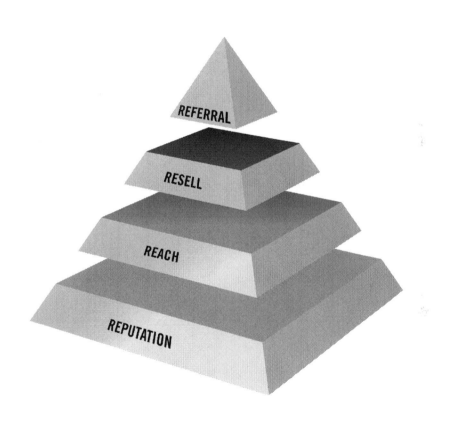

These are the four things Day Spas | Med Spas need to plan for and optimize, to maximize their growth potential. Data shows, and my experience proves, that each of these can account for about 25% growth on their own, and when combined, they have a compounding effect that can ignite growth, up to 100 percent or more.

Let's briefly run through each element and explore how maximizing these 4 R's could significantly impact growth at your business.

*What are you doing to proactively manage, protect and monetize your most valuable asset—your reputation?*

The first R is reputation. As we discussed earlier, it has never been easier for potential customers to find out what others think about your business.

This is both good and bad (depending on what people find). People search online before they buy and we know that they put a lot of stock in what they find and read online. In fact, a recent Nielsen study shows that 74% of U.S. consumers choose to do business based on online feedbacks – even when it's feedback from total strangers!

According to Nielsen's summary of their poll data, recommendations from personal acquaintances and opinions posted by customers online are "the most trusted forms of advertising".

Whether it is positive or negative in tone, most of the content about your business that is available online is not even being created by you anymore! Consumers are critics and publishers now. They all carry tiny "printing process" in their pockets!

## REPUTATION: MORE IMPORTANT THAN EVER

Businesses have always relied on their reputation, but the stakes are even higher today, because of how easy it is for consumers to find information about local Spas before they buy.

**We like to focus on Google reviews and recommend taking a proactive approach to acquire them because of recent changes Google has made.**

Google is often the first point of contact between a customer and a business. From finding businesses nearby, to planning itineraries for upcoming trips, to looking up a forgotten phone number, we plug keywords into Google to help us with anything we want to know. And if we want to find out how one business compares to another, we Google to find out about other people's experiences.

Google reviews are favored by the search engine and show up upon every relevant result, if your business wants to have a good presence on Google, the best place to start is by getting more Google reviews.

## THE IMPORTANCE OF GOOGLE REVIEWS

**Getting reviews from your customers has always been a beneficial exercise for Spa's, but today its importance is even greater.**

## THERE ARE THREE MAIN BENEFITS OF GETTING CUSTOMER REVIEWS

1. *To acquire testimonials you can use in marketing your Spa;*

2. *To better understand your clients' needs and how to serve them better; and*

3. *To improve the visibility of your business on Google.*

## THE POWER OF REVIEW DATA SHOULD NOT BE UNDERESTIMATED.

First, the power of the customer testimonial cannot be underestimated in its influence on other potential customers. You can tell me you are the best Spa in your area, and I may believe you. However, if an unbiased third party tells me you are the best, I'd be much more inclined to believe it. In fact, one recent study suggests that customer reviews are the most powerful purchase influence. Another study found that 88% of consumers consult reviews before making a purchase, and yet another study indicated that 63% of consumers are more likely to make a purchase from a site that has customer reviews.

One hesitation Spas have in soliciting online reviews is the fear of receiving a bad review. However, receiving the odd bad review is not necessarily a bad thing. Actively replying to bad reviews and looking to resolve a situation, illustrates to your new potential clients that you care about your clients.

A study actually found that bad reviews can increase conversion rate by 67%.

## SO, WHY ARE TESTIMONIALS SO IMPORTANT IN AN SEO STRATEGY?

In Google's pursuit to deliver the most relevant and beneficial results for local searches, they not only want to know what your business does but how your business is perceived. They do this, in large part, by seeing how many reviews you have and what your average customer rating is. Want proof? The tour illustrating the features of the new Google Maps states outright that the "highest-rated" businesses near you will be returned when you search with local intent.

Google also recently updated its map search layout, to show ratings and reviews much more prominently. Additionally, with Google, content is king; adding user generated content on your site or your Google plus page is a great way to add new, fresh, and unique content. The quality and quantity of reviews on Google Plus Local, is one of the most important ranking factors for local SEO. And, when a person scans the search results for Spa services in Google, the business listings that include customer reviews present greater credibility and naturally, receive more clicks. If your search result listing shows a 4.5 star rating with 18 reviews (and your competitor listings show less), that's strong social proof that your Spa is trustworthy. Another fact to be conscious of, is that, in today's day and age, your clients will review your services whether you want it or not. Even if reviews are not posted to your site, there are numerous web sites such as Yelp, Merchant Circle, and social media sites where reviews will appear. To maximize the effect of your reviews, and to maintain as much control over them as you can, prompting your customers to leave reviews about your Spa on your Google+ Local page should be a top priority.

Acquiring 5 star Google reviews can be a challenge for the Spa owner so we have simplified this process.

## OUR SYSTEM.

A mobile number is always collected at the front desk. The number is entered into the desktop portal and the client gets a friendly reminder via text message on how to leave a review. There is a shortened link in the text message that takes them directly to a mobile friendly page to leave a review and, a button to publish the Google review. The system sends 3 friendly reminders for those that did not leave a review, and also **redirects** reviews less than 3 stars to a separate internal customer review portal **before** they get published online.

**This one, automated system can potentially save your Spa thousands of dollars of lost revenue due to a negative review getting posted,** because it takes the unhappy client to a page where they can vent their frustrations before becoming a permanent and damaging mark online for all to see. What's more, as we've already discussed, negative reviews can get lodged in the search results, hanging like an albatross around your neck and dragging down sales.

The bottom line is; no matter what system or process you use, taking a proactive approach to not only generate more positive 5 star reviews online, but also keeping the bad reviews from getting published is a wise investment.

## STUDY:

90% of consumers online trust recommendations from people they know;

70% trust opinions of unknown users.

# REACH

*What are you doing to ensure that
more people know about you everyday?*

The second R is reach. It's my experience that a Spa that wants to grow needs to make sure that more people know about it today than they did yesterday.

If you're not meeting new people and telling them about your products and services, if you're not developing a pipeline of potential new customers, you are going to see fewer sales in the future as a result.

This sounds pretty obvious, I know. But I'm always surprised when I talk to Spa owners and ask them about their promotional efforts.

When I look at the pipeline-filling activities of Spas, I see mostly a scattershot approach. A campaign here and there ... with only a vague idea on whether they are getting a positive return on their investment.

No wonder so many Spa owners have become skeptical of marketing; they're doing it wrong!

Very rarely do I see coordinated, systematic and metrics-driven efforts to reach a wider audience and drive more prospects through the front door. Focused, on-going and intentional marketing is exactly what's necessary to reach more qualified prospects in a cost-effective—not to mention satisfying!—manner. A once-in-awhile, ad-hoc marketing strategy is not going to get the results you need to achieve consistent business growth.

The goal of marketing is to make your spa services the obvious choice for consumers searching for solutions to whatever their problem or pain point may be.

Every piece of marketing needs to capture a feeling in them, a feeling of comfort and assurance, that their decision to put their trust in your services is the right move. The key here is to describe that situation to your ideal client, using their own words. When we do this, it resonates with them. All buying begins with some way of getting the buyer to lower their defenses a little, so you can have that consultation with them.

## A PROPERLY DESIGNED SALES FUNNEL WILL:

**Target your ideal clients with marketing that guides them down a path from discomfort to comfort—a comfortable relief gained by buying your service.**

I want you to think about your website for a minute. You probably have a page listing the services you offer. Do you believe this is enough? Is this enough of a draw to get your ideal buyer to interact with you? Maybe you even have pages describing each service in detail. Do you believe this is enough? Listing features and benefits of your services?

Features and benefits become more significant to your client LATER. Not at the beginning. In the beginning of the consumer journey, your ideal buyer is in a SITUATION they want to get out of. They may have pain and are looking for the right massage clinic to treat their type of pain, they may be concerned about wrinkles, and they may be searching for ways to make them feel better about themselves. This is where content marketing comes in.

# CONTENT MARKETING.

A good content marketing plan begins with audience research and the development of targeted messaging. Content marketing applies from the moment someone begins the process of investigation, all the way to the point where they become a client/customer and beyond.

## ALL YOUR SHARED
## OR PUBLISHED CONTENT:

- *Should be a place where consumers can engage with YOUR brand.*

- *Effectively taps into how your buyers want to feel when they use your service to evoke "buying triggers" and emotions in the copy.*

- *Have headlines and images that are crafted for maximum engagement on Social Media.*

All the content published on your website should be developed around your buyer personas. You attract more and more visitors to your website as you write more and more content for your buyer personas and the search keywords they are using.

Think of your content as permanent assets with each new piece building on the overall search effectiveness of your website.

Writing content to the keywords your buyer personas are searching on, performs one of the roles of Search Engine Optimisation (SEO) on your website. This is automatic once your content is published.

Writing good quality content about topics that are of interest can be time consuming. Here is how we perform content marketing.

# CURATED CONTENT.

Curated content is content from other sources that are used on your own branded digital assets. Curated content can be used for brand building and positioning, generating leads, and Social media engagement. It is a great way to position your spa as the expert and authority in the industry and is a huge time saver over having to write all original content.

We first research content on other industry sites and news outlets that have been shared on social media. We then curate the part of the article that we want for our page or post with our clients own image and branding, along with some original content and unique perspective. We use original catchy headlines and images to get attention.

After the article is published on the client's' website, we add a call to action on the bottom for lead generation, and share the post on the client's' social media channels for maximum exposure. The original source of the article is always mentioned on the bottom of the curated post, along with a link back to article.

Curated content done correctly and consistently WILL produce positive results to your bottom line but you want to understand where the traffic is coming from and which type of marketing is generating the highest return. (ROI).

# KEY PERFORMANCE INDICATORS.

| GOAL | SUGGESTED METRICS |
| --- | --- |
| Increase brand awareness | Social media engagement, (likes, comments, shares) email forwards |
| Lead generation | Inbound calls, blog signups, contact form submissions |
| Improve customer loyalty & retention | Social media followers, bounce rate, retention rate |
| Encourage client referrals | Social media shares, comments, follower count, word of mouth |

# SOCIAL MEDIA

## FACEBOOK

Our first choice for quick consumer engagement: Highly targeted Facebook and Instagram Ads.

Posts on your Facebook page are reaching a small fraction of your page "fans" and if you are relying solely on your page fans to engage with your posts without promoting the content, you are missing out.

There needs to be a targeted promotion strategy with every post.

When you're not advertising to discount-seekers, but local buyers of your services, the whole attitude and arrangement has changed. The key difference here is that we get high quality local prospects **when they are looking** for the spa services. We use (and recommend) a highly targeted advertising of a kind, which you may not have known existed until now. Ads targeted to likely buyers of your services—local customers who want what you offer!

**Example: How we turned $100 in Facebook Ads into $26,600 in revenue.**

The goal of this campaign was to generate new client leads for medical aesthetic services.

*Facebook Ad campaign performance graph.*

Step 1: We ran a geo targeted Facebook Ad campaign to a target demographic for these services.

Step 2: We created a mobile responsive landing page that marketed these aesthetic treatments and offered 10% off to increase conversions.

The landing page included:

- *Clear, concise long-form sales copy with easily scanned bullets, headings, and imagery.*

- *Appointment request forms in 3 separate places throughout the copy.*

- *The Spa's phone number, listed in 3-4 areas throughout the copy.*

- *A single, unified, call to action prompting the lead to book appointment.*

Step 3: Prospect calls to book appointment of fills out the appointment request contact form.

**The average client value after upsells was $1,900. The campaign resulted in 26 new leads in 2 weeks. Out of the 26 leads, 14 of them booked an appointment.**

## INSTAGRAM:

**Instagram is a growing social channel and we highly recommend using it.**

There are now over 7.3 million daily users in the US (and counting) using the Instagram application on their phones and once Facebook acquired them, became a great way to build a list of followers quickly. Unlike Facebook, content on Instagram is hard to miss by your followers. Once you get users to follow your brand, they physically have to scroll through your visuals to get to the next image in their feed.

**Using popular hashtags to get likes and followers.**

Hashtags are important to use with every Instagram photo because it's how the photos get organized, shared and valued. Current trends are all affected by the choice of hashtags and will help you grow your followers as well as follow powerful trends. Use your own hashtags to create your own trends based on you service offerings!

**How to use hashtags.**

After adding your image and comments add the #hashtagname in the comment area. To add a hashtag to the image simply add it to the caption field after choosing your filter.

Example: You take a photo of your Spa and it is in Seattle, your hashtag could be #bestseattledayspa or #yourspanameseattle

Sometimes adding hashtags at the end of commentary works best.

Example: Another happy client getting a facial #seattlefacial #seattledayspa

Once you build your followers using hashtags, you can use your own public brand hashtags to get found. Encourage your followers and clients to snap photos for you while using your spa services and have them use the specific public hashtag for your spa like #yourbusinessnamelocation.

# QUICK TIPS:

1. *Follow as many of your clients on Instagram as possible and ask them to follow you back.*

2. *Have regular contests and special offers for Instragram followers, in order to keep clients excited about your posts.*

3. *When your clients post photos of your Spa (or of themselves at your Spa using your services) make a big deal of it. Add their photos to the website, blog, facebook, etc.*

4. *Take photos of your employees and clients (with their permission of course) and link them to your website.*

5. *Insist on hashtags for every photo & brand your own hashtag and encourage your clients to use it with contests and photos. This helps with circulation & branding.*

6. *Get feedback.*

People know what they like and will give you feedback when you ask for it. The more you know what your clients like, the more you can replicate the same feeling and experience.

It is important to convey emotion in the images that evoke a desire within the user to want to do business with you and book an appointment. **The end result is more sales!**

*What are you doing to upsell, cross sell and repeat sell to maximize the lifetime value of a customer?*

The third R is resell. Once you've done all of the hard and often costly work of getting a customer, you need to make sure to maximize the lifetime value, or LTV, of that customer.

Whatever metaphor you want to use... mining your backyard... picking the low hanging fruit... the point is the same; It makes more sense (both financially and from an efficiency standpoint) to fully capitalize on your existing customer base than to be constantly on the hunt for new customers. The more value you can generate from each customer, the less you have to spend on marketing, which means you can increase your profit margins and/or reinvest the savings into your products and services—in the process, making your business even more attractive to your customers! In practice, this can mean increasing the dollar value of each transaction or increasing the frequency that customers buy, either by offering add-on services or upsells or cross-sells.

There are so many cost effective and track- able ways to bring customers back to your business. Let's explore a few:

**Monthly email newsletters:**

The best thing about email newsletters is the ability to reach your client base with information about your treatments on a consistent basis. They should be formatted to represent your brand and they should be crafted to spur emotion and create action. Open rates (about 20%) continue to decline with email however, so having a program in place that maximizes subscribers is essential to keep engagement high. Make sure you have an opt-in form on your website clearly visible from every page and post and clearly state why they should get on your list!

## TEXT MESSAGE MARKETING.

The best thing about text message marketing is the ability to reach over 95% of your mobile subscribers instantly and with average response rates of 20 percent or more, it potentially costs less than a dollar per client in your door!

What is text message marketing?

Wikipedia Definition:

*"Text Message Marketing is the link between online marketing and offline marketing for many companies, replacing email in many ways as the preferred way to communicate with prospects and customers. SMS text message marketing is a permission-based form of marketing, meaning that before a company sends a marketing message to someone's cell phone, that person must have initiated the relationship by opting in to receiving messages from that particular company. The company must also allow someone to opt out of receiving further messages by replying via SMS text message with the words STOP or END, thus taking that person's cell phone number off the company's text message list."*

Text Message Marketing allows you to tap into the wide spread popularity of text messaging. People keep their mobile phones with them at all times, giving you unprecedented access to your customers.

The general concept is the same for most Text Message Marketing campaigns. You get people to opt-in to your "mobile VIP-list". They do this by texting a code to a phone number that is set up through a Text Message Marketing company. You can then send text messages to the people in this list. The more client mobile numbers you have, the more of them you can expect to book an appointment on short notice, based on your openings. You can use this for offers, deals, coupons or just to stay fresh in the minds of your potential customers. A list of 300 mobile VIP members can easily attract 10-15 new clients in a day with the push of a button!

# RINGLESS VOICEMAIL:

Ringless Voicemail also known as direct voicemail messaging is a new, non-intrusive way to reach new prospects and past customers with personal, mass messages that get them calling you to book an appointment!

A Few Advantages of Ringless Voicemail:

- *No interruptions to customers because there is no ring.*

- *More likely to reach the targeted prospect.*

- *Allows for professionally produced, customized messages.*

- *Adds a human touch to mass marketing messages.*

...and its 100% FCC Compliant!

90% of adults have a mobile phone and 67% of those find themselves checking their phone for messages, alerts or calls even when they don't notice their phone ringing or vibrating!

The increase in the use of mobile phones has resulted in the decrease of traditional communication methods, which makes it more difficult for those still relying on those traditional methods to connect with people, to gather and share information.

# THE CATCH 22.

Current laws regulate who can call us directly on our mobile phones, which is great. After all, who wants to hear their cell phone constantly ringing?

Here is the catch 22. If people are overwhelmingly using their mobile phones to communicate and yet current laws restrict the ability to contact cell phones, then how are your clients going to receive key information about your specials, new treatments and services, events, etc.?

This is where Ringless Voicemail comes in. It is a cutting edge technology designed to reach target audiences within minutes of sending. The clients we have on our system have had response rates as high as 12%.

Imagine the ability to drop a voicemail message directly into the recipient's voice mailbox, without ever making a call or ringing their phone line. There is never a charge for a call to the subscriber and the system 100% legal! It is classified by the FCC as an "enhanced service" and is designed to be a non-intrusive form of communication.

*Despite having easy access to new and cool tools, most Day Spas in our area are leaving money on the table because they're not maximizing the resell potential of each customer.*

*What are you doing to use your successful relationships to create new, organic opportunities so that you can spend less and make more?*

The fourth R is referral. Since you're doing such a great job taking care of your customers and keeping them happy, the next best thing you can do is set up systems to maximize the benefit you get from them, right? So that they are doing the marketing for you!

Well, it's well known that if you just leave it up to people to do referrals for you, very few will—even if they are very happy with you.

You have to make it very easy—almost effortless—for your happy customers to refer your business, if you really want to maximize the referrals you generate from them. A study from Lee Resource Inc. found that attracting a new customer can cost five times as much as keeping an existing one.

## REFERRALS MAKE GREAT CUSTOMERS

We all want referrals because they help us save money on marketing, right? Well, there's even more to gain from referrals than cost savings:

According to a case study noted in the Harvard Business Review, customers that come from referrals are, on average, about 18% more likely than others to stay with a company and they generate 16% more in profits!

And according to several case studies reported on by the website, TechCrunch:

Friends referred by friends make better customers. They spend more (a 2x higher estimated lifetime value than customers from all other channels) convert better (75% higher conversion than renters from other marketing channels at Rent the Runway); and shop faster.

## WHY ARE REFERRALS SO POWERFUL?

Because they channel the power of social proof; Social proof is a fancy way of saying that we humans are easily influenced by each other.

We're pack animals. When a member of our pack (family) or tribe (social circle) recommends a product or service, we take that recommendation very seriously. Similarly, when someone in a position of power, prestige or authority recommends something, we are very quick to act on that recommendation.

You see the applied power of social proof everywhere: in TV ads, when you see a celebrity endorsing a product; on the radio, when the person hosting the pledge drive tells listeners that so-and-so donated $50 to NPR; on the back of a novel you're reading, when you see testimonials from other notable authors; and on the web, when you visit sites like Yelp.com to read consumer reviews of local restaurants.

## MOVING FROM PASSIVE TO ACTIVE, AD HOC TO SYSTEMATIC

Almost without fail, most businesses I talk to, have no clear referral generation system. And the reality is that referrals don't just happen, you have to go out and get them! And if you're going to spend the time collecting them, you need a system that effectively channels your efforts into tangible results.

# THAT'S IT...
# FOUR SIMPLE SYSTEMS
# FOR GROWTH!

Growth isn't complicated. But that doesn't mean it's easy, either.

The reality is that, the majority of Spas are operating without a plan to maximize these four systems, or they aren't even aware that they exist. The day-to-day activities of operating their business leaves them with too little time and energy at the end of the day to master the fundamentals of marketing or keeping up with the latest technology innovations.

## IF YOU'RE READY TO MAKE A SHIFT,

You may realize that you need to make a change, that you aren't growing like you should, that your current approach to marketing is not working, and that you are committed to getting past your current income limits. If so, I would be interested in talking with you to see if there is potentially a good fit for us to work together.

We are particular about who we work with.

We work with businesses that are already successful and are looking for strategic ways to get FAR MORE successful.

We work with clients that have the mind-set and resources to handle the level of growth that is possible to achieve.

## WHAT TO DO NEXT

*If you've seen the benefit of what you've read in these pages, then I'd encourage you to contact us immediately. From there, we will set up a follow-up phone call interview to see if we are a good fit to work together. This phone conversation is not a guarantee we will work together. But it is a necessary first step, if we are to work toward achieving the growth you're capable of!*

## HOW TO CONTACT US

### Pick a method, any method:

- Phone: (206) 569-8586

- Email: jeremy@jtbinternetmarketing.com

- Website: jtbinternetmarketing.com

**We look forward to hearing from you!**

*Now on to the interviews....*

# 25 INDUSTRY
# PROFESSIONAL
# INTERVIEWS

To listen to the audio recordings of these interviews, go to:

http://dayspamedspasuccess.com

# AMANDA GORECKI RN.

*Healing Waters and Pure MD® Skin Science*

Jeremy: My guest today is Amanda Gorecki, Amanda is an advanced registered nurse practitioner and founder of Healing Waters and Pure MD® Skin Science. She has a BSN from Seattle Pacific University and an MSN from the University of Alabama at Birmingham. Amanda trained at Harborview Medical Center and Duke University where she worked as an emergency room nurse and nurse practitioner for the Department of Neurosurgery before venturing into private business. Amanda was named Enterprising Woman of the Year in 2014 by Enterprising Women Magazine; she is an Atlanta member of the WPO (Women's Presidents Organization) Chapter 1. She received the Champions of Respect Award from the YWCA Women's Shelter, has been nominated for the Ernst & Young Entrepreneur of the Year, and was named one of the 40 Under 40 by the Wichita Business Journal.

Amanda founded Healing Waters in 2002, twice named the Best Medical Spa in the Country, and recipient of numerous local awards for Best Spa, Best Massage, and more. Healing Waters currently has locations in Wichita, Kansas; Durham, North Carolina; and Columbia, South Carolina.

In 2007, Amanda pursued one of her greatest passions by developing the proprietary skin care line, Pure MD® Skin Science. All Healing Waters spas offer customized Pure MD® facials and retail products. Gorecki is regarded as an expert on skin care ingredients and has lectured nationally on cosmeceuticals at various women's conferences nationwide.

Amanda continues to dedicate her time to the development and expansion of both Healing Waters and Pure MD®, with a focus on growing the company's mission of inspiring transformational change in the lives of others. Gorecki's ultimate goal is to make a difference in the lives of others—to help people find their self-confidence and to feel good about themselves.

Jeremy: Welcome Amanda.

Amanda: Thank you.

Jeremy: What inspired you to open Healing Waters Med Spa?

Amanda: Well, my husband and I had worked for years, more in trauma and neurosurgery and emergency care, and we saw all these people that would come in all the time and just have appalling circumstances in their lives. We just felt like if we could get to them sooner, if we could get to them sooner and help them to make positive lifestyle choices.

There're so many end-stage diseases that come from smoking or alcohol abuse or drugs, and there's a lot that can go on in someone's life. Someone who has a brain tumor or gets something by accident, and you ask yourself what it takes to wake up with it daily. However, most of the time, it stems from our lifestyle choices, and so our real goal in beginning Healing Waters was to create a place that was beautiful, relaxing, inspiring, that would also help them make positive, healthy, lifestyle choices so that they could live a more fulfilling life.

Amanda: I grew up in the Northwest and literally grew up on the beach because there was so much water everywhere in the Northwest. It was not a luxury thing to live in the Northwest, and because we were surrounded by so many peninsulas, water was such an integral part of my life. We wanted to create a place of healing, to create a place of positive lifestyle choices, and so we came up with the name Healing Waters, and it stuck, and it's now a success.

Jeremy: What do you like most about the work that you do?

Amanda: I would say one of my favorite things about the work that I do is getting to inspire my leaders and my team members, and then what they do is to multiply it and encourage our guests and our patients. So my work is more integral to the team members and the leadership and even just right before talking to you. for instance, I was on the call with one of my leaders, and she was struggling with a team member, and my first thing was "sit down, talk with her, have a conversation, give her what you're looking for, help her succeed." What I found is we have so many team members that have been with us for ten years, 11 years and they will say I've become a better person from working at Healing Waters, so I found when the team member becomes that better person, they multiply it with their guests.

Jeremy: What are some of the most popular services that you offer?

Amanda: Our Pure MD Facial is one of our most popular services. We worked hard to combine excellent ingredients, extraordinary interventions in the facial but it must also be relaxing, and so people come in and say my skin is so much better but I go for the relaxation of a massage with my facial, and so we stay solidly blocked with our Pure MD Facial. And then I would say our Body Ritual, our Healing Water Body Ritual, between those two services those are our most popular.

Jeremy: Are your clients getting great results from those treatments?

Amanda: Absolutely, yes. I would say the Pure MD Facials; somebody will come in and say not only did I get a chance to relax, but my skin is also brighter, my skin is softer, it's clearer, and I feel better. And then, especially taking the home care products home, they're able to continue what they got in the spa daily at home.

Jeremy: That's great. What makes your spa unique? What makes it stand out?

Amanda: I would say I would just go back to our mission. The crux of our mission is to inspire transformational change. Whether it's on a small basis or a large basis, we do everything at our facility from manicures, pedicures, massage, facial to extensive plastic surgery. We do them all with excellence, and so when a guest comes into our facility, he/she will see we're working to inspire a transformational change. Whether it's helping them feel better about themselves, less depressed, through the spa services or helping them through breast cancer, if we were able to do breast reconstruction for them.

By having a mission that our staff really can get behind, it becomes deeper. It's more about making a lasting difference with your guests, and people will say all the time, «What do you do to make it so great here?» I even work at a distance from my locations. I work out of Atlanta, and our locations are in the other states, and they say what are you doing to make a difference, and I say it's our mission. It's not just words on a page.

We breathe life into our mission every single day, and so one of the touch points we have is twice a day we have a daily huddle, and it's a requirement to go to the huddle. In the huddle, our purpose for the crew is not just to give information, but it's also to re-energize our mission, every single day. What we find is that our staff will say not that I just love working at Healing Waters, but I don't ever want to leave Healing Waters. I love being a part of this.

I encourage them that this is your business. It's not just my business; this is your business. They come to work, and they feel like it's sometimes the best part of their day, and if you can get team members to feel like work is the best part of their day, that's huge, and so it transfers over to the guests.

Jeremy: Excellent...Having a real strong collaborative team environment that's dedicated to the mission, that's wonderful. I take it, that is part of what you would attribute to your success to?

Amanda: Absolutely, but literally you've got to breathe life into it every single day, and you've got to treat it as if it's a business decision. It's got to be as much of a business decision as reconciling your bank account, and so we treat it as if it's a business decision. I have weekly meetings with all my managers, and we start our weekly meetings off with our inspiration, and our inspiration is always tied back to our mission and our core values. When that's something that's the heart of your organization, people can get behind it; they feel the difference, and then they act out the difference.

Jeremy: What's your biggest challenge right now?

Amanda: I would say we have grown so much. We have three locations now all in different states, everything from extensive plastic surgery to entry spa treatments. It's very important to me as we head into 2016 to stabilize and get more consistent in every piece of our organization before our next growth. So in January this last year, we opened a new location within a hospital system in South Carolina, and the largest hospital system in South Carolina bought the rights to our company to put on the ground floor of one of their new hospitals. That was a big growth opportunity, so I'm looking to re-stabilize for our next growth time.

I'm always looking to climbing up the mountain, and when we get to a valley, we'll keep climbing and then stay up there as we've reached the peak of our mountain, but now we're re-stabilizing before we hit that next mountain that we're to climb.

Jeremy: You're affiliated then with the hospital system?

Amanda: Yes, Palmetto Health out of Columbia, South Carolina, decided they want to put a spa in their organization, and they met with us, and they bought the rights to use our brand and all of our operating systems for ten years within their hospital.

Jeremy: How often do you communicate with your clients? Via e-mail? Via text? Via newsletter, social media et cetera?

Amanda: Daily, daily, daily. I mean we are on all forms of social media, so between Twitter, Instagram, Facebook, every day there's something we're giving to our clients, and then I would say twice a week we do e-mail blasts to our clients, and so with our marketing, we're always on television. We always have a consistent marketing presence, but as far as directly communicating through social media outlets, it's daily.

Jeremy: Do you see any of your clients making mistakes when coming from other spas?

Amanda: Yes, we'll see that every once in awhile. Someone will say I got a Groupon, and I went somewhere else, and they'll come back to us to fix it or whatever. I would say one of the things Healing Waters is known for in this industry is that it is a volatile industry. We've been in it since 2002 and never wavered. We have the same ownership since 2002 and in some places the same leadership that we've had since opening. Even if people veer off, they'll come back. Because we worked hard to get the recipe down and so the recipe is very, very, very consistent, but I can tell you it takes from the top down staying very healthy, staying very positive, and staying strong to keep that consistency up. And I can tell if my stress load gets too much, I can't be who I need to be for all of our team members.

Jeremy: Are there any services that you're offering now that you wish more clients knew about or took better advantage of?

Amanda: Often we are the market leader in our area, so if we do a service we'll have somebody else copy along right after us and try to do the same sort of thing. We work really hard to stay focused and not look to the left or right. We want to make sure we do price checks quarterly or around just to make sure we're staying very competitive. We don't want to be the most expensive, but we don't want to be the least expensive. We want to hit that sweet spot, and so most of all of our services, yes, our competitors jumped right on the bandwagon right away right afterward. Then we just always make sure that we're doing it the best.

Jeremy: Can you describe an ideal spa client?

Amanda: I would say an ideal spa client is someone who values themselves, and values making an investment in themselves. I wouldn't always say that our ideal spa client is somebody who has lots of money because I've seen somebody who may be more average income level, who actually will invest more in themselves than a very wealthy individual, so an individual who values and understands the importance of investing in themselves.

Jeremy: What do they want to accomplish?

Amanda: One of the things that I say all the time is it's not just about what we look like on the outside, it's how we feel on the inside. It affects our marriages, and it affects our children, and If I am strong in my interpersonal areas and my emotional, spiritual and mental health, I'm a better wife, a better neighbor, a better mother, and a better businesswoman. I can do all of that better whereas if I get off kilter, then I'm not able to be who I want to be.

Jeremy: Someone that's looking for a more holistic approach, not just necessarily a quick fix?

Amanda: Right.

Jeremy: That's great. Well, that concludes my questions here, but before we end, I want to give you an opportunity to let the readers know anything else about your spa.

Amanda: We'd love to have them visit us. We'd love any feedback on ways we could improve, and we hope to have an opportunity to invest in them. We look at it as not just someone coming to us, but it's what we can do for them. Our website is: healingwaterslife.com/

# BARNEY NELSON

*Massage Envy*

Jeremy: My guest today is Barney Nelson. Barney attended Roanoke College and received his BBA degree. He then began his career in high tech sales and worldwide sales management including 17 years with Intel Corporation. He also helped develop Intel's e-business capabilities. Barney was introduced to the Massage Envy franchise opportunity via a broker in 2003 and then signed on with the Massage Envy franchise in 2004. He is now the regional developer for the State of Washington and oversees 17 franchisees that own 28 locations. Welcome, Barney. It's great to have you with us today.

Barney: Thanks, Jeremy.

Jeremy: I'm interested in your perspective on the franchise model in this industry. But before we get into that, what made you interested in buying a massage franchise?

Barney: Well, franchising was of interest to me because statistically franchises tend to do much better and last longer, and they tend to be more successful as opposed to a "do it yourself" start-up type of company. With franchising you have people backing you up, you have proven systems, training, there's a safety net of support in place, and that along with the brand equity that has been built up really helps to franchise a much less risky proposition. History has proven this out. The less risk and support appealed to me at that point in my life.

The massage was something that also appealed to me because I've always liked getting massages. But then part of it was also realizing that it's actually a 3,000-year-old industry, traced back to China; that had never really been organized. It has also been a highly fragmented, multi-billion dollar industry. Around 7 billion dollars per year in 2004 and it is very rare to find a multi-billion dollar industry that is also so fragmented. At that time, most of the providers were small "Mom and Pop" shops, and that presented a unique opportunity.

And then also the fact that I saw massage as a for fast growth industry as time goes on. There's a big baby-boomer demographic out there, and I'm one of those people, and we're getting more aches and pains as we get older. The demand for massage has continued to grow as a result of that. The mainstream acceptance of massage therapy continues to grow in the US and it will never be replaced by technology, nor can it be outsourced to some other country. So all of those foundational things came together and convinced me rapidly that this would be a heck of an opportunity to be involved in.

Jeremy: I take it you have been successful with it?

Barney: Yeah, it's been very successful. It was the right concept at the right time. The whole idea of combining a membership dues type of model with massage therapy, and then going nationwide, was revolutionary. However, there are three main words that capture what we are trying to do at Massage Envy; professional, convenient, and affordable. We are very convenient; we're open seven days a week, roughly 90 hours a week. And we are now in 49 of 50 states and your membership benefits can be utilized at whatever Massage Envy you go to providing a high level of convenience, which was one of the founding characteristics of this company that is crucial.

Jeremy: Did you start with just one location?

Barney: No, the first franchise I sold licenses to opened the first two locations in the Seattle area within one week of each other. Later in 2004, I opened my own location. And so by the end of 2004, we had opened up three locations in the State of Washington. That was very fast and exceeded our expectations.

Barney: And from there it just continued to grow. Once we got the first one open, people could see for themselves the beauty of the model and the potential. They could look around, they could get a massage, and that clicked and resonated with many people. So I sold many franchises pretty rapidly, and we brought them all on, and now we're at 28 open locations.

Jeremy: How did you become the regional developer? Was that a title that you had early on or did that just title grow as the locations grew?

Barney: Well, a regional developer can also be called a master franchise in some examples. I bought the license for the State of Washington making me the regional developer, and that license gave me the opportunity to sell the franchises, bring franchisees in, and then get paid based on royalties, and commissions for selling franchise licenses. I'm not selling new franchises very much now because we have so many locations open, and there's not a lot of room for more growth. So that's kind of how that came together.

Jeremy: Can you talk about the Massage Envy as a brand and why you feel it's been so successful?

Barney: First of all you're in a growing industry. It's the rising tide, and it lifts all types of boats, and that is huge. The mainstream acceptance of massage therapy just continues to grow, more and more people are now seeing it as a viable element of their wellness routine, and we very much are a value oriented type of play by making massage available to more people and making it more affordable.

The founder of the company went around and talked to a lot of people before founding the company regarding what they liked and didn't like about massage therapy. And they all said that....

every single person said ......they would get more massage if it were more affordable. So we make it more affordable and in turn, the volume then goes up. People who are getting one, two, or maybe three massages a year are now getting a massage a month and sometimes even more than that.

So we came in and enabled that, and we've grown the industry a lot as a result. And we've hired a lot of therapists, and we have over 600 massage therapists working for us in the State of Washington. So by far, we are the largest provider of massage therapy in the State of Washington and the entire country, and we've done over 80 million massages in the history of the company.

Barney: So I think it was the right concept at the right time.

Jeremy: I noticed from the website that Massage Envy is now branching out into facials, offering facials.

Barney: Right.

Jeremy: And I also know that there are different types of massage services available, so given that, and because you are now branching out and offering facials, what do you see as the most popular service that's being offered right now?

Barney: Massage continues to be our most popular thing that we do, and the lion's share of the services that we provide are massages in various modalities. Swedish massage, deep tissue massages are two of the bigger ones, treatment work. We have people coming to us that have migraine headaches for example, and they get a massage every week, and as a result of that, they no longer are having migraine headaches.

Our facial business though is about the fact that we are a wellness-oriented company. We have a total wellness type of package that we provide to our customers, and that's where the facials come in. We focus on the elements of facials that are really more about skin care, and we don't currently provide beauty related services. It's not a cosmetic type of thing; it's more about wellness. And we have an exclusive arrangement with Murad to use their products, which are very fine products, which we sell and utilize when treating our customers. So that's why we have also expanded into the facial and skin care industry.

Jeremy: What do you think makes Massage Envy stand out from the competition?

Barney: Well, we are the first ones to do this kind of model, the dues-based model nationwide around this professional, convenient, and affordable type of mission statement words if you will. So we had first mover advantage and continued to have that. Now, we do have some copycat/imitator type of competitors that have come on that have copied the same thing that we're doing. But if you add all of them up together, their locations that they have opened don't even equal 20% of the amount of locations that we have opened. We have opened over 1200 locations. So we have taken advantage of first mover advantage type of idea. That has made a big difference for us. That and the quality of our massage therapists and estheticians.

Jeremy: What is your biggest challenge now?

Barney: Well, the biggest challenge is maintaining and managing the growth that we have. And from that standpoint unless we have enough massage therapists we can't continue to grow. So we are spending a lot of time working with massage therapy schools and people in the industry cultivating relationships. We're offering scholarships to students at the schools to help promote not only our name but also assist them. So that's been one of our biggest challenges lately with all of the tremendous growth- continuing to find qualified, really capable massage therapists.

Jeremy: How often do you communicate with your clients? What type of communication systems do you have in place...email, Facebook, social media channels, Instagram, text messaging, etc.?

Barney: Yes, we do all of that with our customers. We do email, and we have Facebook fan pages both on a national level and at the location level. We have a Twitter account, we send out tweets on a regional basis, we have a blog that we operate, and we also have a Facebook fan page that we started which is not necessarily Massage Envy; it's more for the entire massage therapy community. It's called Massage Therapy Careers in Washington, and we've received about 3500 likes in a very short period.

So we reach out in a lot of different ways, and we have a full-time local marketing agency that works for us. We're always looking for ideas, things we can do. We have done broadcast radio in the past. We continue to do Pandora Radio; we find that to be pretty effective because it's a little more targeted than just basic broadcast radio. We have done some TV advertising in the past. We're not really doing it now. And we've headed more towards digital social media options.

Jeremy: You mentioned the type of problems that clients will often have before they come to you, whether it's pain or stress, and some of the treatments that you offer to help. Is there any service now that you're offering you wish more clients knew more about or took better advantage of?

Barney: Well, I think our facials and skin care are things that we're looking to continue to grow and get the word out. That's a newer thing that we've done in the last four or five years. So there's still some room for growth there. And of course, what sometimes happens is we have customers that will get a massage and a facial during the same visit, which works out well for them and they end up feeling quite relaxed and content. So that's kind of a growth area for us.

And beyond that, massage therapy is just a growth industry, as I said before. It's quite interesting and amazing how much it has grown. It is now, at least, a 10 billion dollar industry. And again I go back to the fact that there's a large demographic of people that are getting older and, therefore, more inclined to try something like massage therapy as mainstream acceptance grows.

In some ways, i believe the United States in the past lagged behind the rest of the world, particularly Europe and Asia, in understanding the benefits of massage therapy. But I believe that the United States has mostly caught up. I honestly believe that we were one of the people that helped make that happen.

Part of the reasons why the United States lagged behind in understanding the benefits of massage therapy, I believe, was there was nobody really at a national level to plant the flag, if you will, for massage therapy and really educate the public. And that's something that we're doing. You'll now see Massage Envy commercials on nationwide TV for example. That's been going on for some time now.

So it still continues to grow as an industry and it's a lot of fun. It's the kind of business where customers come in, happy to be there because they're getting a massage or facial, and end up leaving even happier with the treatment they received.

Jeremy: Absolutely. What percentage of them that are walk-ins end up signing for a monthly service agreement?

Barney: Around 30% of our customers that are not currently members end up signing up for our Wellness Program, approximately. And then sometimes people will sign up and then decide they don't want to continue, but then they'll come back and re-sign up.

Jeremy: They miss it, of course.

Barney: Yeah. We typically have 25 or 30 massage therapists and estheticians at every location. And so we almost always guarantee that we can find one, two, or three of them that will probably be a good fit for your situation and that you will appreciate and like. And once that bond is in place between yourself and, at least, one massage therapist or esthetician, the massage therapist or esthetician gets to know your situation, knows what to work on, and what works best for you. It kind of helps cement that whole relationship and tends to make it a very long-lasting relationship. We have many customers who have been with us for ten years or longer.

Jeremy: Great to know.

Barney: And one of the great things about dues based model, financially, by the way, is that the dues come in each month. Most other businesses are subject to whoever walks in the door that particular day, determining whether you're going to make any money for that day. When you're in a dues-based model like a gym business, for example, there will be dues coming in every day whether people come in or not. Now we always really encourage people to come in and utilize their member benefits, including reaching out to them very regularly and inviting them in, but the dues model is beneficial from a financial standpoint.

Jeremy: I get it. Okay, we're about out of time. But before we end I want to give you the opportunity to explain to our readers and listeners anything else that you'd like us to know about Massage Envy.

Barney: Just that we are always trying to be the most customer service oriented company that we can be. And that's vital to us as you can understand being in the business that we're in. So if you give us a try, we have an intro massage or facial at a reduced rate. Just try it and see if the therapist or esthetician works out for you and see if we provide for you the help you're looking for.

We will spend time working with you, understanding what you're trying to accomplish and what your points of pain are, what your needs are, and then we customize for you based on what you need. So when we hit that right, we end up with very, very happy customers, and that's what we like.

Jeremy: It's been wonderful learning more about Massage Envy and your background and your part in its success especially in the State of Washington. So thank you very much for your time

# DR. BEN KILLEY

*Blue Haven Med Spa*

Jeremy: My guest today is Dr. Benjamin Killey. Dr. Killey has been practicing emergency medicine for the past ten years. He was trained at Southern Illinois University School of Medicine, did his internship at The University of Chicago and his emergency medicine residency at Cook County Hospital in Chicago. He began practicing in the Puget Sound region in 2007. He received his training in medical aesthetics from the American Board of Aesthetic Medicine and completed and passed the board certification course.

Dr. Killey has always believed in pursuing multiple interests in life. He received a bachelor of music in piano performance from Illinois Wesleyan University in 1999. While at IWU, Dr. Killey was the 1997 MTNA collegiate state champion in piano for Illinois and was named the top graduate in the school of music at graduation. He continues to perform concerts today. He was also featured on the television series Untold Stories of the ER on the TLC network in December 2010. He is currently singing with the Seattle Men's Chorus. His favorite hobbies are volleyball, tennis, running and reading. Welcome, Dr. Killey.

Ben Killey: Thank you for having me.

Jeremy Baker: It's great to have you with us today. I'm curious.... What inspired you to become a med spa owner?

Ben Killey: I've been asked that question a few times. I still don't feel like I have a great answer for it, except that, I was practicing full-time emergency medicine and I still practice full-time emergency medicine and was looking to do something else in addition to that. I had heard about cosmetic procedures years ago, and I didn't know what it would take to get trained to do those procedures. I was not familiar with them, but I'd heard from another co-worker who was thinking about doing it that they were thinking about getting trained to do those procedures. I started looking into it.

The more I read about what can be done, non-surgically, for cosmetics, it was kind of exciting to hear about it and read about the different procedures. I've always been very procedure oriented; using my hands so I thought that would be a good fit for the things that I'm good at and the things that I enjoy doing. The more I thought about it, the more I decided to do some basic business planning and thinking about the feasibility of it. Eventually, it got to the point where I was ready to go forward with it and decided to go and get trained. I went to the American Board of Aesthetic Medicine and did my training there. I was really excited about it after that. It was a great learning experience. From there, I decided to go ahead and open the business.

Jeremy Baker: Okay, so you opened this spa in what year?

Ben Killey: 2011.

Jeremy Baker: How did you arrive at the name and the location?

Ben Killey: The location was a bit of a process. When I first started, I did a lot of business reading on my own to decide how I wanted to run my business and what are some of the best practices that have worked. What I decided was that I was going to start small and do kind of a starting location and practice on friends and family initially until I got comfortable with running a business and working out the kinks and things like that. It wasn't until I had run the business for about three years that I decided to expand and then move to the perfect location in Green Lake.

The name Blue Haven was a brainstorming process over the course of weeks. Where that eventually came from, I had been reading all kinds of books on how you name a business. How do you advertise yourself? Some of the principles that resonated with me were using a color in your name because they've shown that people can remember a color much more easily than they can a word.

I knew I wanted to have a color in the title. I knew that blue was the color I wanted, it's not just my favorite color, but it's also the number one favorite color of both men and women worldwide. I decided to include that in the title. Then it became an issue of brainstorming what would go well with the word blue.

That was the hardest part. I came up with all kinds of names, and it was just a process of narrowing them down, eliminating ones and eventually I got to my top three or four choices and emailed them to ten or twenty of my good friends, across different demographics and asked them to vote. Blue Haven was I think the second most common number one choice but for the people who didn't vote it number one, they voted it number two. The one that had the most number one votes amongst my friends were also the last choice for the other people who didn't vote it number one. I decided to go with the one that was less controversial and less likely to be disliked by someone.

Jeremy Baker: What do you like most about what you're doing now?

Ben Killey: I like being an entrepreneur. I like being able to build my business the way I want it to be built and the way I want it to run. I can choose the team that I like. I'm really happy with the team I've selected between my office manager and the other doctors and my esthetician. I felt like I was able to choose the best people and those I believe will work well together. If there's something I dislike about the business, I can change it. It's not like, past experiences where you've been an employee, and you can't do much about it.

It is something where I can make my own decisions. I do a lot of analyzing of other businesses about what makes them great and what I like about an experience when I go to another business and then I can apply those principles to my own here.

Jeremy Baker: What's the most popular service that you offer right now?

Ben Killey: Botox. Botox injections for sure.

Jeremy Baker: Okay.

Ben Killey: It's not just our most popular; it's the most common cosmetic procedure worldwide.

Jeremy Baker: What do you think makes your spa stand out, make it unique? What do you think is special about it?

Ben Killey: I believe that it comes down to the knowledge base and procedural skills of the people working. Advertising only goes so far. You need to produce results. You want people to be happy with the results. Everyone that I've got working here, we're all very committed to staying on top of what's current and what's the most up to date and safest options available. That's the motto of my business. I'm trying to stay in the forefront, whenever new things become available, like when newer techniques come out, more modern equipment that might be safer with less risk of various side effects; I'm going to pursue that. I want to find out what that is. It's difficult to learn a new skill. It's uncomfortable at first. You've got to make that commitment to do doing it.

Jeremy Baker: Your technical aptitude and keeping on top of the latest techniques and procedures, would you consider that attributable to your success?

Ben Killey: It's definitely part of it. There're so many aspects of what makes a business successful. That's one of them, one of the aspects that contribute.

Jeremy Baker: What would you say your biggest challenge is now?

Ben Killey: The business is only four years old, we're still in that growth phase. It's not growing too quickly, growing at the appropriate rate, but at the same time growing enough where it becomes a viable business, and it's staying healthy and you're getting word of mouth referrals to keep things going.

Jeremy Baker: How often are you communicating with your clients? Regarding social media, email, text, etc.?

Ben Killey: We have an email list. We send out monthly specials. I think once a month is kind of my limit on how often I want to tell people about what's going on. It's usually in the form of, "This is the special we're running for the month." If people are looking for a discount on something, we're offering something to them. For the most part, people contact us when they're ready for the re-dose of their Botox or whatever. That's about the extent. We do have a Facebook page of course and have a website we keep updated.

Jeremy Baker: Do you see any clients that come from other spas, or had aesthetic treatments elsewhere, that are making mistakes that you have to solve?

Ben Killey: We have seen some come from other spas and then for whatever reason decided to try us, whether it's a word of mouth referral. But with non-surgical treatments, Botox or filler's there's not a whole lot where you would reverse something. If someone had a terrible Botox job, there's nothing you can do, but it wears off in three months. That has not been the case where someone comes to me for repairing something else. That would be probably more in the surgical world.

Jeremy Baker: What services or procedures do you offer that you wish more people knew about?

Ben Killey: There are a couple things. The one thing that I think we're providing those other spas do not provide would be the treatment for thinning hair. There is now an FDA cleared device called the Laser Cap, and we are the exclusive dealer for the Pacific Northwest who sells it. It's an at-home device that you wear every other day for thirty minutes, and it stimulates the health of the hair follicles and then ideally you're preserving those follicles and restoring some of the thickness to the hair. That is probably the one thing that we're exclusive to.

Regarding other unique qualities, I guess, we were one of the first ones who were using the micro cannula for filler use which has, I think, completely revolutionized filler injections. The old method is to inject repeatedly using a needle with filler which is painful and there's a lot of bruising and swelling involved with that. Micro cannulas came about relatively recently, and that was a technique that took some practice to get perfected, but now that I've done it, it's completely changed. Filler procedures are not nearly as uncomfortable as they used to be. There's such a reduction in swelling and bruising and downtime with the micro cannula. A lot of people are coming to me for that reason that has had filler injections previously, and it was a bad experience because of pain. They are amazed at how pleasant filler can be.

Jeremy Baker: How would you describe your ideal client? Concerning what their situation is, what they're looking to accomplish and how you can deliver that.

Ben Killey: I mean there are so many situations out there. I don't have particular ideal clients, but what I am looking for it someone who has a realistic goal for non-surgical options which is looking to improve their appearance non-surgically. I think it's all about expectations. Here's what Botox can do, here's what fillers can do, here's what lasers can do. If people understand the goals of those treatments and that's what they're looking for, then that's an ideal candidate.

I tried to boil down what we do into three categories. There are three categories of aging that we deal with here. Category one would be, developing wrinkles because of muscle bulk that occurs in our muscles of facial expression. That's what causes our frown lines, those horizontal forehead lines, the crow's feet. That's where Botox has its role. It's weakening those muscles to reduce the lines that are caused by that.

Category two, are changes of aging due to loss of volume in the face. For example, the fat pads that we have in our cheeks and mid face go away as we age, and then we get kind of a sunken, hollow, tired look. That's where fillers have their roles. You're replacing that volume. You're inflating the tire, is how I kind of think of it.

Category three would be the changes to the skin itself on the surface. That's where there's a pretty wide variation of what you can do. You can remove pigment deposits that have left spots. You can remove veins or red dots called cherry angiomas. You can improve the quality and texture of the skin and make it smoother and firmer. There are many ways of doing that whether it's a laser resurfacing in the face, or doing chemical peels, or getting regular facials with microdermabrasion to stimulate the new skin. That's where there's probably the widest variation in the terms of options available.

Jeremy Baker: It's fascinating, what's available now in terms of choices and products in the medical aesthetic world.

Jeremy Baker: Is there anything else that you'd like the readers or the listeners to know about you and your spa?

Ben Killey: Well, I would say that if they have any questions or if they're interested in seeing what I would recommend for them, we offer free consultations. They should feel free to call and let me analyze their face and talk about what I think would be good options for them. Our consultations are free of charge. http://www.bluehavenmedicalspa.com/

# CHRISTINE POYTHRESS

*Christine Face and Body*

Jeremy: Today, I'm talking with Christine Poythress. The owner of Christine Face and Body located in Mercer Island, WA. Christine has been a licensed Esthetician since 1990. She has worked in Downtown Seattle and on Mercer Island. In 2008, she opened up her skincare studio on Mercer Island. Christine is interested in new technology to enhance one's skin and keeps current with skincare trends with education and research. Some of Christine's specialties include Anti-Aging Treatments, Micro-Current and Hydrodermabrasion technology, Youngblood Mineral Cosmetics, Acne treatments and Brazilian waxing. When not working in her busy skin care practice, Christine enjoys being a mother to her daughter Leila. She lives on Mercer Island with her family.

Welcome, Christine.

Christine: Thank you for having me.

Jeremy: The first thing that I would like to know is what inspired you to become a spa owner.

Christine: Well, I don't know if it was as much inspiration as just need. I started my business because my daughter was just being born, and I have been an Esthetician for almost 20 years by that time, but have always worked for other people and thought it was just time to do something for myself and create my own space to work out of. That's what I did. That's when I created Christine Face and Body.

Jeremy: How did you go from being an Esthetician to starting your own business?

Christine: Well, I don't know if there was any secret formula if that's what you're asking. I just saved my money and used what cash that I had and tried not to get myself into debt and just took all my skills as an Esthetician and my clients just continued to follow me and continued to come in. I barely had any product. I just had a table. So, I just kept on working. I didn't give up. I just kept working through the transition and making the best choice that I could financially by not spending a lot of money, doing things on the down low. I think we were at the beginning of the recession, too. So that was about '08. A lot of salons were closing in the area.

Jeremy: Not easy to do. A lot of them did close especially the single operator businesses. Do you have employees?

Christine: I do. I have one and a half employees and also, an independent contractor that works for me. Her name is Ms. Nancy Meadows. She has been quite a mentor to me. I started working for Miss Nancy Meadows back in 1992 when I first got my aesthetics license in the state of Washington. I was living downtown. I was 19 years old, 20 years old. I wanted to live downtown and work downtown. That's when I found Nancy Meadows Skincare and Makeup. I worked for her for seven years.

Jeremy: You consider mentor's as an important part of your business growth, and having that network of support around you?

Christine: Yeah. She's great. She's been an Esthetician for nearly 40 years. She's got a great reputation around Seattle. By that time, when I started working for her, she was already 20 years into it. So, I was working with somebody who had a vast clientele, did very little advertising, and is still doing that work today just because it's what she likes to do. She's created these long-time friendships and business relationships with clients that she doesn't want to let go. She's still here today with me too. She works only two days a week, and only takes her long-time clients. I don't give her any new clients. I've been seeing her for the last 30 years. That's a great inspiration for me.

Jeremy: What do you like most about the work that you do?

Christine: I think I like most about it is being physically busy. I'm kind of a busybody. I like to be on my feet. I like to be moving. This job, what I do, is like that.

Jeremy: Makes time go by faster.

Christine: Yeah. It takes a lot of time. I see people sometimes for 15 minutes, 30 minutes, sometimes and the hour on the hour schedule. So, to keep things running smoothly, we need to be moving quickly and swiftly. It's fun because you do make friends along the way. I love making new friends.

Jeremy: What are some of the most popular services that you offer?

Christine: I do a lot of anti-aging skincare. I do a lot of acne skincare because I had acne as a teenager and in my 20s, so I'm kind of an expert in that. I do a lot of body waxing. Brazilian style waxing is very popular here. It's one of our specialties. I've been doing that for 20 years. It's quick, it's clean, and it's a popular treatment for me here.

Jeremy: What do you think makes your spa stand out or makes it unique from some of the others that are around the area?

Christine: It's a community....and my experience. I think I have a lot more experience. I'm going on my 26th year in skincare. I take a lot of classes. I think it's the education. I keep educating myself. I love education. I like telling people about things, reading about products, why they work, why skincare works. I think it's the training and the experience.

Jeremy: Great. What do you think your biggest challenge is?

Christine: My biggest challenge now? As a business owner?

Jeremy: Yes as a business owner.

Jeremy: Running the business, the daily operations of the spa, everything from the actual technical application of it, to the marketing, to anything you can think of. What would you consider your biggest challenge?

Christine: I think right now the biggest problem was income tax returns and estimated taxes. That was a big challenge this year. When you make more money, you pay more money out. So, financially, that would be the biggest challenge this year: how much more I had to pay towards taxes. Not trying to get on my soapbox, but taxes for business are excruciating. The second biggest thing would be finding good staff. Finding responsible, reliable people that want to help you grow the business. I think that's a big challenge for me right now. I have the clients for certain treatment areas like massage therapy, which we offer. Because I am trained as a massage therapist, I'd like excellent massage therapists. It's hard to find somebody who runs their massage therapy practice that they do as a business. Because I would love to find someone like that. But it's a challenge in that department. The primary problem would probably be advertising and marketing. Putting those dollars towards that and finding what works.

Jeremy: How often do you communicate with your clients?

Christine: Every day, when they come in once a month. Our regular, great, long-time standing clients come in every month. I communicate with them every month. I communicate with them via email as well, when they schedule their next appointment, and we send them a text message and an email confirmation. We connect that way. I send out thank you cards to clients who spend a lot of money or referred a friend, or they're going through something. I try to reach out to clients on a personal level sometimes too.

Jeremy: Are there any mistakes that you see either your clients or other people make when they go to the spa for skin care services?

Christine: I would probably say watch for good sanitation practices. That's super important. That would probably be the number one thing. Certain skin conditions, diseases that are out there today, they're very easy to pick up. You have to be clean. Gloves, sanitizer and that kind of stuff. That would probably be my number 1.

Jeremy: So you mentioned anti-aging as one of the leading services. How do you address aging skin?

Christine: Well, we have some particular treatments that work well for aging skin. I work with the Dermalogical skincare line. Its many different segments of products for all types of skins. They have an anti-aging line, and it's called "Age Smart." It's super effective, and it uses different acids and vitamins. My clients that I do that a lot on, those types of treatments, and have them on good home care that has a lot of vitamins in them, and educate people about staying out of the sun; that's the number one. Super sun-damaged, aged skin needs to be on a good regimen that has lots of vitamins and lots of mild exfoliators, and regular treatments. Coming in and having regular treatments.

Another tool that I have, which I use and is great for anti-aging is called Hydro Facial. It's by a company called Edge Systems. Right now, Hydro Facial is probably one of the number one pieces of technology out there right now. It's exfoliation, with hydration. It drastically changes people's skin, whether it's acne or aging. We use that a lot. It's a quick, water-based treatment, and people love it. People get great results. That is probably my number one tool, right now, against aging skin. My weapon.

Jeremy: Describe your ideal client.

Christine: The ideal client comes in with an open mind, and doesn't fuss, isn't too high maintenance, and lets me help them figure out what it is they need to do.

Jeremy: What would be the first step that you would want them to take?

Christine: Yeah, because often, people are drastically aged or have acne skin, I naturally refer them to a dermatologist, to a physician in the area. I have a couple that I work in close collaboration with that I have been referring to regularly, or see for my skin concerns. I don't think that I am a miracle worker. We're not doing heroic skincare over here. I'm just educating people. Helping people look, feel better about themselves. Helping them protect themselves, and look better with good skincare.

Jeremy: Great. Is there anything else that you'd like the readers to know or the listeners to know about you or your spa or your services?

Christine: No. We're on Mercer Island. We have great skincare. Great staff. We're open late, here until 7 pm most nights on Mercer Island. We're really good. Caitlyn is one of my employees. She's fabulous. She's a goodie. She's great with waxing and makeup. If you want to makeup, I just bought a new piece of equipment. It's called a Lamp Probe. And with a Lamp Probe, it uses radio frequency. So, radio frequency is used a lot actually to change the skin on the surface by electro cauterization. Burning away tissues like skin tags.

Christine: It actually will burn things off. Burn moles, burn little cherry angioma's, help them to diminish, using these small probes. So, I'm pretty excited about that. That's coming in the mail soon. I should be getting that today or tomorrow. We're going to start training for it. We're going to start offering treatments and services for clients for these little, tiny things like skin tags, where you would normally go to your dermatologist. They could just come to me.

Jeremy: Wow that sounds exciting.

Christine: It's interesting. I have wanted this piece of equipment for a long time, but like I said, when you try to make your purchases wisely and not get in over your head with finances and debt, great things happen. You can buy new pieces of equipment that you've wanted forever.

Jeremy: Well, that's great. thank you for taking the time to go over these questions and inform me and the readers and the listeners about your spa. It sounds interesting. It's been great speaking with you.

http://christinefaceandbody.com/

# DR. ALISHA MOADAB

*Reday spa*

Jeremy Baker. My guest today is Dr. Alisha Moadab. Dr. Alisha found herself interested in medicine but didn't want a prescription pad as her only tool. During her first term in undergraduate school at Portland State University, she enrolled in an intro to pre-med class. Her first term, where she was introduced to an array of healthcare professions, it was there that a naturopathic doctor explained the medicine to the class while serving tea and Dr. Alisha says it was like love at first sight. From that point on, she knew that this was the medicine that she wanted to practice. Being born and raised in Portland, she was fortunate to have the first and to found a naturopathic medical school in her backyard; it's called the National College of Natural Medicine, NCNM. She served as a student ambassador both at PSU and NCNM where she fundraised to help NCNM community clinics for the underserved population. Dr. Alisha has a passion for combining beauty and wellness. She lives in Temecula, California and enjoys the sunshine, reading health and personal development books, staying active and her family. Her motto is, "If you don't have your health, what do you have?" It's great to have you with us, Alisha.

Alisha: Thank you so much, Jeremy. It's a pleasure to be with you.

Jeremy Baker: I have questions about your naturopathic practice in general, and how you decided to offer the aesthetic services. But why don't you just give us a general overview of your practice to start with.

Alisha: Great. So for people who don't know what a naturopathic doctor is, imagine going to a primary care doctor and, like you said, the current model is often a prescription as a remedy and we all know that a pill for every ill is really not the best way to go about health. When you visit a naturopathic doctor, you get to have extended time with your visit. A new patient visit is about an hour long, and then follow-ups can be anywhere from the 30-45 minutes in length. So a naturopathic doctor's goal is to incorporate the entire body; so not just excluding digestive systems like that, but also asking about how, maybe, their mental health and their levels of stress are. In my practice, I see all types of health concerns, whether it's the common cold, to cancer and everything in between, whether it's hormonal complaints, digestive complaints, etc.

Jeremy Baker: What was your inspiration for opening up your practice and a sub-part to that is your motivation for offering aesthetic services?

Alisha: When I was in medical school -- I graduated in '09 and in the years leading up to that I started noticing these places called medispas popping up and I was just really intrigued by them, I was, just seeing it as a very popular thing at the time and I thought, "You know, women often go to fixing the outside first." You know, you look in the mirror, and maybe you see something that you're not happy with, and you address that first. Maybe you're not addressing, though, the fact that you're exhausted, or you're having some other health problems, but your first thing is, "Well, if I look better, maybe I will feel better." And so in my mind, I thought, "Wouldn't it be great to have a place where women can go and fulfill those exterior needs, whether it's, you know, doing a filler or a muscle relaxer like Botox, but then also get the education about how beauty really comes from within," and I really wanted to marry those two, so to say. And I was blessed that a family friend had a medical spa in Portland, Oregon and when I was graduating and finding where I wanted to set up a practice, I had the opportunity to partner with her, and I've never left, kind of, the industry, so to say.

Jeremy Baker: What typically comes first in your practice? Do your patients come in because they're not feeling good, and then they see the aesthetic services are part of your practice and then have you provide those, or vice-a-versa, or is it a mix of both?

Alisha: It's somewhat a mix of both. I would most likely say, though, that it is the aesthetics that is most likely to get them in the door and it is when they are on the treatment table and I am performing an aesthetic services that I may say, "You know, I'm noticing that your thyroid may be off because I'm seeing that your eyebrow hair is now-- that you're losing some, and that's a sign that we can look for to see if other things are going wrong." You know, the body is a great messenger, so if you know what to look for, whether it's the health of their nails, the color of their eyes, the pattern of acne lesions that can give us about hormonal balance. So when they're in the chair going for that aesthetic service, I try to look at those cues and then gently kind of start a dialogue of, "You know, I do offer a free 15-minute consultation if you do want to talk about your health." So that's generally how that process goes.

Jeremy Baker: So offering those aesthetic services has been a good way to generate new clients/patients?

Alisha: Absolutely. And on the flip side, - if somebody's coming for me for health, unless they obviously say something in their appearance bothers them, it's my personal preference not to bring it up, and I think the spa setting is a great way, though, to have cross-referrals, so that is another way that patients will come to me, aesthetic or for health concerns. So for example, we do offer pedicures here. So if somebody is in the pedicure chair, and maybe they're complaining about their appearance or the way they feel, if I've done my job and educated that nail therapist to have the ability to talk about my services, then that person could refer me and schedule that complimentary consultation for that client.

Jeremy Baker: I can see how that can be a good way to generate some new business and also help new people. What do you like most about the work you're doing now?

Alisha: Oh, I think what I love most about what I do, is the opportunity to help change the way people think. I love to incorporate the mental health and emotional side of both the aesthetics and the medical side. When a woman is in my chair, and she's talking about her crow's feet, her facial lines, etc., and maybe we are performing Botox, I will, as a sideline, actually give them homework. If I kind of clue in that she's maybe talking poorly about herself and I'm sensing there is a, maybe, a lower self-esteem or they're just very critical of themselves, my homework assignment is for them to look in the mirror every day and give themselves a compliment-- whether it's, "I love my beautiful blue eyes," or, "I love my luscious lips," and that kind of thing. And on the health side, maybe it's not looking in the mirror and giving yourself a compliment, but it might be expressing gratitude, you know, having them write down three things that they are grateful for every day. I find that our mental health really does kind of impact, you know, the way we see ourselves and the way we feel.

Jeremy Baker: Great advice. What would you say is the most popular service that you're offering now?

Alisha: Within my scope, right now we're kind of in a season where lots of people are fighting colds and cases of flu. I do something called IV therapy; it is a mixture of nutrients, like Vitamin C, B vitamins, other minerals like calcium and magnesium, selenium, and we put this in a push, or an IV bag and people will have increased immune capabilities as well as feeling relaxed. It's great for athletes, as well, chronic fatigue, sinus problems, allergies, and even things like fibromyalgia. So IV therapy, there's a common formula called the Myer's Cocktail, and that's a precise formula that will deliver those nutrients that I mentioned and just has people feeling really good. The next day they will, you know, maybe kick that cold or just feel their energy-enhanced.

Jeremy Baker: How long does that take?

Alisha: An IV push, if it is done in the push format, might be a 20-minute push, and then if we are putting it in a bag and dripping it, maybe 45 minutes to an hour.

If somebody needs something even quicker, I will give them an intramuscular shot of a blend of B vitamins. I like to use not just B12 alone, but adding B5, B6, and B-complex. We know that these are the nutrients that help nourish the adrenal glands and the adrenal glands producing cortisol, helping with our energy levels, as well as modifying stress and balancing out the hormones and neurotransmitter support. So that can be an IM injection right into the hip, and then I love, also, offering glutathione. Glutathione is our body's most potent antioxidant, and we make it; however, if we're under a lot of stress or coming across a lot of, kind of, insults to our body with an increase of free radicals, we need more antioxidants on board, so you can give glutathione intramuscularly, as well as intravenously.

Jeremy Baker: Interesting. Your naturopathic approach makes your practice/spa unique. What else do you think makes your spa unique and stand out from some of the competition in the area?

Alisha: I think that we are a-- I call it a 'one-stop shop' in that you can come here and do a little bit of everything, health included. So, you know, for a woman or a man who needs to get their hair done, their nails, their facial, their massage, maybe they want a steam room to kind of loosen up those muscles, and then maybe they need that pick-me-up with the IM injection, or maybe they've been lax about getting blood work done. I do draw blood here, so literally what I think is great about re-health is you can come here and only drive to one location and get all of those services and your needs met without driving, you know, this place and that place for your, you know, health and wellness.

Jeremy Baker: That's a nice advantage that you have, being able to offer wellness treatments as well as aesthetic treatments.

Alisha: Yeah, when I think about it, you know, we're all so pressed for time and, you know, to find the time to drive to appointments, even, can add up; so that's what I love about being here. And of course, the cross-referrals, too, of just us all being a team player and wanting to see our co-workers and colleagues succeed.

Jeremy Baker: Yeah, that's great. So you have been successful; what would you attribute your success thus far to?

Alisha: That's a great question. I think perseverance is a key to success. So, you know, I look at it like as a roller coaster and there's a lot of ups and then there's the valleys and the downs and I always try to look at those, you know, those adversities as an opportunity to grow and an opportunity to see, "How can I make this system better?" so to say. So, you know, right now I'm in the process of trying to get systems down for our front desk and the whole spa operation. You know, being a small business owner, you're starting from scratch, so to say, and so you don't always know the proper way to do things, and I think just being able to repeat something and make it a systematized model is going to be really beneficial for our continued success. And I think just working with a great group of people is crucial to any spa owner. You know, it's an industry where getting a group of, largely, a group of women together, it can be great if we're all aligned and wanting to adopt that 'growing everyday' mentality.

Jeremy Baker: What is your biggest challenge now?

Alisha: That is a great question. My biggest challenge... I would say it is when you are the operator, as well as a practitioner yourself; there comes a balance of how your run your day and your weeks and your time to give the appropriate amount of time to each responsibility. That's one of my struggles right now of when do I put on which hat, so to say. And then my goal is also to just kind of have the place always be a tranquil and serene environment-- so sometimes getting different contractors into, you know, maybe updates paint and the cosmetics of the place.

Jeremy Baker: Keeping that warm, tranquil environment and also keeping it updated.

Alisha: Yes. We are blessed that this Spa is a family-owned business, owned by a prior family, and it's been in Temecula for ten years now. So it's great to have that longevity that my critical eye, if you will, kind of sees, "Oh, I really want, you know, this nice kind of updated remodel look," and just trying to do that in pieces and phases.

Jeremy Baker: How often are you communicating with your clients via email, text, social media, etc.?

Alisha: We communicate via text for our appointment confirmations, which has been a really valuable tool, so I highly recommend that if somebody's not already doing it.

Jeremy Baker: Are you doing that on a point of sales system?

Alisha: We do, we use Millennium. Their spa edition, I feel like, it's great. So it's through that platform that we were able to do the text confirmations.

And then we use constant contact currently. We're sending an average of, I would say, one email per month. To be honest, our social media is a source of where we need to kind of ramp it up a little bit more. So for now only an occasional Facebook post.

I would say that we lack in that, and I can't wait to see, you know, our growth when we can get those systems dialed down. Currently, I am a member of BNI, which stands for Business Networking International. That's how a majority of my business comes to me, is through referrals.

Jeremy Baker: OK, great. Great. Yeah, I'm a member of a networking group as well. They can be a great source of referrals.

Alisha: Oh, it's amazing.

Jeremy Baker: Do you see clients making mistakes when coming from other spas?

Alisha: Well, the first thing that came to mind is when somebody is seeing me for Botox and when they've been going elsewhere. The maker of Botox, Allergan, has a program called Brilliant Distinctions and I do see that as an industry issue when we're not, kind of, going the extra mile for our clients, in that maybe the client who's now seeing me has been getting Botox for years-- or maybe not years, you know, even just a few times-- and they've never heard of Brilliant Distinctions and maybe I should, for anybody who doesn't know what Brilliant Distinctions is, I liken it to a frequent flier miles program. So you fly on an airline, and then you go online, and you say, you know, you get points and then points equals' rewards. So with Brilliant Distinctions, if you're a provider order Botox from Allergan, it's no cost to you; you basically go online, and you enter your vial number and, an issue that treatment online and then that generates points for the client, which translates to dollars off their next treatment. So to date, I am really proud to say that I have saved my clients in the last, approximately, close to four years, approximately ten thousand dollars in, you know, coupons related to getting discounts on their aesthetic treatments, whether that's Botox or Juvederm and Latisse.

Jeremy Baker: Interesting.

Alisha: But do I see any other errors from other providers? Sometimes, you know, I have known to be more of a conservative injector as far as let's go in with fewer units, having the approach that I can always add more and I would rather have under-treated than over-treated.

And I see – I hear that depending on who's injecting, you know, if you are – if you're the injector, and maybe you're getting paid a commission and getting paid per unit, there can be a conflict of interest, so to say, of wanting to offer that client more units than, perhaps, they need. So that is something else that I am mindful of, you know, of really wanting to do what's best and in the client's interest.

Jeremy Baker: Great. What service are you offering now that you wish more of your clients knew about or took better advantage of?

Alisha: I would like to say my naturopathic medical service. I think that many people don't know their vitamin D levels, and yet we know that vitamin D is related to heart disease, as well as cancer-- #1, #2 killers-- and I wish that everyone knew where their vitamin D, their cholesterol, etc.-- had some basic blood work, see how their thyroid was functioning. So I wish that you know everyone who's walking through a medical spa took the time to, as much as they're investing on the external, of investing as much or greater on the internal.

Jeremy Baker: Wonderful advice. Who would you consider to be an ideal client for you?

An ideal client is a woman in her I would say mid-forties to mid-fifties who is going through that change of life. Hormonally, they may be experiencing hot flashes; they may not feel like themselves anymore, and I love to nurture them and get their hormones back in balance and then also help them feel better about that external.

So maybe it is, you know, doing a little bit of Juvederm so when they look in the mirror, they do feel better about themselves. Or the common thing is, you know, clients being told from other people, "Oh, you look angry," and it's their glabellar lines are coming through. I take the time with every Botox client to ask them, "OK, you have these glabellar lines, let's think about why are you frowning? You know, is it your face of concentration or is it because you are squinting to see?" And I will then refer them to a local optometrist to get their eye exam done. Having the approach of, you know, what is the causation and trying to treat the cause of even their aesthetic problems.

Jeremy Baker: That's about it for the time that we have for this call. But before we end, anything more you'd like us to know about your practice? What's your website, so everyone knows?

Alisha: We have two websites, so DrAlishaND.com and redayspa.com and you know, what I'd like everyone to know is that I have a philosophy of giver's gains, so if you guys need any support, have any questions, am open to helping anyone I can.

Jeremy Baker: Wonderful. It's been great learning more about you and your practice, and what you do and your approach, and I like your overall approach. So I wish you the best and continued success and a wonderful rest of your day. Thanks again for being on the call with us today.

Alisha: Thanks so much. It was a pleasure and honor, and I really appreciate the opportunity.

# DR. VERN REYNOLDS.

*Elite Body and Laser.*

My guest today is Doctor Vern Reynolds. Dr. Reynolds has an extensive background in the med spa industry as a physician and is now opening his spa in Columbus, Ohio. Dr. Reynolds graduated medical school as a board certified anesthesiologist and is currently a board examiner for graduating anesthesiologists. He's also involved in sports medicine, and is currently on "The American Board of Ringside Physicians". He's the doctor for UFC and MMA events, boxing events, bodybuilding, and fitness shows. His knowledge based on pharmacy and medicine has given him a broad base of hormone replacement therapy, and comparisons of the deliveries of the hormone replacement therapy, meaning injectable vs. platelets vs. topical, etc...Dr. Reynolds has a long history of working with injectables including Botox and various fillers. His new spa which will be called 'Elite Body and Laser' is scheduled to open this May 1st Welcome Dr. Reynolds.

Dr. Reynolds: Thank you

Jeremy: It's an honor to have you with us today, and I'm excited to learn more about your background, and the med spa that is soon to open, and my first question for you is, what was our motivation for getting into medical aesthetics field from anesthesiology?

Dr. Reynolds: Twofold, I'm a single father, and I have my children the majority of the time, and the on-call was killing me. I was taking so much on-call at nights, I was always exposed to other subsets of medicine, and have experience as a ringside physician, the bodybuilding, the fitness, a lot of the cosmetic field, which I was introduced to while being a medical practitioner there, people came up to me, about a laser burn, some wrinkle control that was not done correctly, too soon or too slow, and people ask me for my opinion, so I slowly learned over the years how to recognize certain things, and began to take coursework to do that myself. I have a background in art, one of my undergraduate pursuits was in art medical illustration, as well in pharmacy, I have a pharmacy degree, I'm a pharmacist as well, and It allowed me to focus on different approaches, I guess when these questions were presented to me by these athletes, whether these questions were nutrition based, hormone based, cosmetic based, I began to educate myself and take coursework so I could deliver some answers to them. So for the past several years I have evolved my skill set. I'm an athlete myself and continue to live by example I guess, and perform these abilities as well, both as a competitor and as a physician. So I relate to these people and kind of know what they are after, I think, that's what I'll bring that's a little bit unique, actually I live by example.

Jeremy: It's a unique experience set, and when you open a med spa in May, you're going to offer a suite of services. Can you list some of these services you plan on offering right out of the gate?

Dr. Reynolds: Sure, we have linked up with a company Cynosure, one of the leading laser companies that bring proven technology. The big one that we like is the upgrade from the cool sculpting, which does a very efficient job, a very nice job, but it can be a little rough on people, a lot of patients will complain afterwards because the way it works it freezes the fat which is cumbersome, take some time, uncomfortable, afterwards you have to massage or rub it vigorously for about 25 minutes, a little bit rough, people complain days and weeks later sometimes. There is a new machine called the 'Sculpture', which is basically the same technology or the same effect used with laser technology .so now we will be able to apply pads to the stomach, non-invasive and these lasers are, very efficient, and will deliver the same perimeter of activity, with no massaging, and half the time with up to a 25% increased effect. So that's something we offer the patient that takes half the time, no massaging the treated area, no discomfort afterward. So quick & easy, with half the downtime.

Jeremy: What have you and your partner discussed regarding the grand opening strategy and the overall brand strategy?

Dr. Reynolds: Cynosure is helping us with some initial marketing. We're having a big grand opening for our new location, and we are going be a trainee for Cynosure. So they are going to send a lot of docs in the Midwest to train with us as well, so they have a vested interest in us as we have an interest in their equipment. So it's a mutually beneficial arrangement. We are planning a pretty good size grand opening and will be marketing to our target demographic for the event. So we are teaming up with some marketing people and radio stations to help us sell the grand opening and then go from there.

Jeremy: Sounds like you are pretty excited about this, what do you like most about what you are doing now?

Dr. Reynolds: I would say it's truly in the medicine; this is something where I can make somebody happy quite quickly. Often people coming don't like visiting their doctor but people are usually excited about coming to see me, and they are more excited when they leave. Even younger girls are doing simple Botox fillers for the first time are a little bit nervous, I don't want to look funny, I don't want to look weird, they leave with a smile on their face, we get texts, we get e-mails, thank you doc. We are so happy. I get compliments all the time, and it's a nice feeling. Everybody is leaving with a better spirit.

Jeremy: What will make your spa stand out from competition in the area? Can you describe what your real unique strategy is in the marketplace?

Dr. Reynolds: I would say for us, with the name "Elite Body and Laser" we want to convey the message that it's not just cosmetics, not just laser, we really focus on the body as well, like I said, will be offering hormone replacement therapy as well and as a pharmacist, I did study on hormones as well. Now HRT is a little more widespread, more acceptable, the target audience for that are the middle-aged people, people coming in with complaints of chronic fatigue, tired, poor focus, low libido, painful intercourse, a lot of things that, you know 50, 60 years old people that are just accepting as part of growing old. They longer have to. In the past few years, there have been amazing advancements in hormone replacement therapy, we choose bioidenticals, the most natural form and that's what most patients want today, more natural approaches, there's injectables, topical creams, but we now offer pellet insertion of the bioidenticals that come from a natural source, nothing synthetic, there's minimal side effect due to the fact that they're the hormones naturally produced in the body. So it's more natural and effective. The restoration of your hormone levels, and the true balance of those, truly achieves great feelings, and it's immediate. The response is immediate, you don't have to wait weeks or months, within a week or so, people are coming back like 'wow, thank you so much', so patients that came in for aesthetic treatments and opted for the hormone replacement therapy, leave feeling better in general. They look good and feel good.

Jeremy: A more holistic approach is certainly a trend that I see in the industry and it's great that you will be able to offer that, treating not just a way that they look, but also the way that they feel, that's a unique distinction in the industry. So you talked about some of the ideal clients, can you expand on that a little regarding what their situation is, what they are looking to accomplish, and how you go about delivering that for them?

Dr. Reynolds: Sure, I serve a diverse group. From athletes, that know what it's like to work hard, to feel good, to the aging population, which is losing energy. A lot of them come in and say 'doc, I don't feel good, I don't focus much, I have no sex drive', and this can start as early as the forties and fifties. Many of these athletes have been my patients since their twenties and thirties, so I've been exposed to the pro athlete demographic for many years as a pharmacist, and as a physician, and now we have different opportunities for them. So one of our targets is your former athlete, your middle-aged 40 years, 50 years that are still active and want to continue to be active. There are a lot of people that still, at that age, are doing marathons, iron, they're doing extra crazy things, but it's also for the spouse, you're the mother of three who works, or stays at home but is tired, "I'm just tired. All day the kids are going to school, I'm tired when they get home, and I'm taking a nap during that day", kids come and need you, your kids, then run you down. They come to me because they are tired. 7 to 10 days after they come in they refer two or three friends, family members. I mean they marketed my services better than I can because they are living proof. As more people see this or sell this, they participate in it. And when they're there as we mentioned before, we have great family staff, all people are satisfied, very nice people, and most of them are patients themselves one way or another, we have younger girls, we have middle age men and women who use all of our services, so they can only lead by example. So the target audience is anybody, anybody that is aging.

Jeremy: I think that's going to be a big advantage for you going forward, especially because now you can open it up and serve, what I consider to be an under-served market, and that's males wanting aesthetic treatments. You get them in the door for treating low energy levels, and they end up getting an aesthetic treatment. Men do get Botox and fillers. So there is potentially a big opportunity for you to get them in the door in the first place, and then offer them these expanded aesthetic services as well.

Dr. Reynolds: Exactly, right

Jeremy: We are about out of time, but before we go, is there anything else that you would like our readers and listeners to know about your spa, your services, any particular service, this is the opportunity before we wrap this up.

Dr. Reynolds: Sure thank you, I would just like to add as well, what separates us from other spas, is our knowledge base, specifically the look- feel good part. Apart from just looking good, is truly feeling it. Somebody can come in, and have cosmetic work done, but if they just don't feel well, it won't last long. Once you get them feeling better, without any other interventions, they have a glow around them, and they feel great. We have fifty; sixty years olds coming in living who once just accepted their tired feeling as a fact of the aging process, and after getting hormone replacement therapy, they're out golfing, playing tennis every day. They are out living life, and you see a certain glow about them, now they take more pride into themselves. So don't forget about both, your inner beauty, and your outer beauty, we treat both.

Jeremy: Excellent, that's a great way to wrap it up. I guess at this point; you don't have a website?

Dr. Reynolds: It will be Elitebodyandlaser.com and should be open here very soon. We are working with the tech staff as well, as we speak.

Jeremy: Ok, Elitebodyandlaser.com, Vern, it's been a privilege and honor speaking with you, and learning about your background, and your upcoming med spa, so best of luck going forward with that.

Dr. Reynolds: Thank you.

# DR. ELLIOT HIRSCH.

*Hirsch Plastic Surgery*

Jeremy: My guest today is Dr. Elliot Hirsch. Dr. Hirsch is board certified Los Angeles plastic surgeon, who practices in the San Fernando Valley. Dr. Hirsch's primary office is in Sherman Oaks and treats patients from not only Los Angeles but from all over California and beyond. Dr. Hirsch practices the full spectrum of plastic and reconstructive surgery, including minimally invasive cosmetic surgery techniques, and state of the art micro surgical reconstructive techniques including muscle sparing, breast reconstruction, and nasal reconstruction. Dr. Hirsch grew up in West Lake Village Los Angeles and attended prestigious John Hopkins University in Baltimore, Maryland where he graduated with a Phi Beta Kappa and Omicron Delta Kappa honors, wow. And also received the Curt P. Richter award for outstanding research in the field of Behavioral Biology.

After his undergraduate studies, Dr. Hirsch returned to Southern California for Medical school at the Keck School of Medicine, at the University of Southern California, where he graduated with the highest distinction and was elected to the Alpha Omega Alpha honor society, as well as the Order of Arete. Dr. Hirsch completed his integrated plastic and reconstructive surgery residency, at the prestigious North Western Memorial Hospital program in Chicago Illinois, where he received several awards for his research in teaching. Since entering medical school, Dr. Hirsch has been an active researcher in the field of plastic surgery, and has co-authored over 40 manuscripts and book chapters, and has received several grants for original research projects, and holds patents for wound care devices. Dr. Hirsch is board certified by the American Board of Plastic Surgery. Dr. Hirsch it is an honor to have you on the show today.


Elliot: Thank you for having me, my pleasure.

Jeremy: I'm excited to learn more about, particularly your unique perspective on aesthetic services being offered, and their rise in popularity. But before we get started with those questions, can you just give our readers and listeners just a general overview of your practice.

Elliot: Sure. My practice is located in San Fernando Valley; actually, we are in Sherman Oaks, which is almost in the geographic San Fernando Valley, which attracts patients from all over the valley, and also Los Angeles, Beverly Hills, and the surrounding areas. We see a variety of patients, not only cosmetic patients but also reconstructive patients as well. And I have an esthetician who works with me in the office, who also performs a lot of our cosmetic non-surgical treatments.

Jeremy: Obviously on the surgical side you're well versed. Can you talk about some of the non-surgical procedures that you offer?

Elliot: Sure. We perform injectables with Botox, Juvederm, and others, and we also offer also chemical peels. There are multiple levels of peels that we offer, and facial treatments with nutraceutical oxygen facial treatment, as well as other facial both by dermatological and other nutraceutical lines.

Jeremy: What would you say right now, either on the surgical side or non-surgical side is the most popular treatment that you offer?

Elliot: Well on the nonsurgical side Botox is always popular. I think the trends that I see in Botox patients are coming younger and younger, for treatments. They want to not only treat existing wrinkles but also to prevent or minimize the risk of further wrinkles, developing over time. So I think Botox is my number one non-surgical injectable. We've also had a big increase in our Oxygen Facial line over the past 2 or 3 months. More and more patients are coming in for Oxygen facials nutraceuticals. I think it's a great product. It hydrates the skin. It can help with acne, and I think it's become more popular for us because multiple celebrities have been talking about how they use it for big red carpet events. That always trickles down to who we see as well.

Jeremy: When did you open your practice?

Elliot: The practice opened about two years ago.

Jeremy: What do you think makes you unique, and stand out from some of your competitors in the area?

Elliot: I think that the cornerstone of our business number one is customer service. The overall experience for the patient from the time that they come in, to the time that they undergo their treatment, or their surgery and then follow up, is we've really put a lot of emphasis on making sure they have a top notch experience. That is emphasized by me, with my staff. I think patients realized that when they come in, and they are greeted by me, they are offered coffee. We go out of our way to make them feel comfortable here. I think far on the way that's number one. What's makes us a little more unique, beyond most of the other people who have similar types of practices are the other services we perform, the reconstructive procedures. There have been multiple patients that I have worked on over the past two years, who undergo not only a cosmetic procedure but also reconstructive procedure as well. So a patient who comes in for breast reconstruction procedure may also want to get the facelift, or may undergo a chemical peel, or injectables. So I think that by providing a top, top level customer service to patients, they feel comfortable with us and ultimately stick around in our family, and undergo the other procedures as well.

Jeremy: Great. Patient satisfaction is the most important thing. It's nice to have those happy patients so they can refer more patients, and more business your way.

Elliot: Always.

Jeremy: What would you say your biggest challenge is at this point?

Elliot: I think there have been times over the past year or so, especially as our business increased exponentially and we have more and more patients coming in. I think that a challenge for the staff is to continue maintaining their high level of customer service, even when we have 30, 40, 50, patients coming in on a given day. So we work on that constantly, and everything that we do is geared to that, so these are just growing pains

Jeremy: Would you say that some of those challenges could be met by additional staff, for just simply more effective procedures?

Elliot: We have hired additional staff when necessary, specifically for that purpose. A lot of it too is just optimizing our flow and making sure that we are efficient with our office practices. So we're not duplicating work, in that everything that can be done during the office visit is done. So that when the patient is completed, that everything is taken care of, and there's no additional work to be done, move on to the next patient.

Jeremy: How often do you communicate with your clients? Social media channels, email, text, etc.

Elliot: With our patients once they come in for a procedure, they meet me, meet our esthetician and also meet our patient coordinator. After the consultation, if they are not undergoing a procedure that day, they will be in contact with either the esthetician or the patient coordinator, depending on the type of procedure. The esthetician will follow up with them as often as is necessary until they make their decision about the procedure.

I know there are patients that have a lot of questions, and they have multiple emails, and I give all of my patients my email. So they can email me directly if they have any questions. Once they undergo the procedure, we want to make sure that they are doing well, and having a smooth recovery time. So again there's a lot of phone calling, emailing afterward. Regarding social media, we are expanding our social media presence, and we are usually on Instagram, Snap chat, Facebook, and a YouTube channel, at least once or twice a week if not more.

Jeremy: That's important. It's good to know that.

Elliot: Absolutely.

Jeremy: Mistakes that you see clients making when they are undergoing treatments, at other facilities. Can you describe them and how you approach the situation differently, or how you correct those mistakes?

Elliot: One thing that I infrequently see with Botox is symmetry. There are times when a patient comes in who's had Botox somewhere else, and they have perhaps one eyebrow is moving a little more than the other eyebrow, and that's a pretty straight forward fix. It just requires a little more Botox above the eyebrow that's moving more. I would categorize that as more of a technical problem. Or sometimes there's more diffusion on one side of the Botox, than the other side. The only thing that I see frequently is more of a philosophical difference. As a board certified plastic surgeon, I endear more towards surgery rather than injectable treatments. So I see patients come in with neck lines and things that would make them stand up to me as being a candidate, for a facelift or a neck lift. They often have undergone injectable procedures at other places, to try to camouflage these findings, and they aren't happy with them. So again a philosophical difference between myself, who is comfortable performing facelifts, versus somebody who does just injectables, or they may try to mask the sign of aging by injecting additional volume into certain areas. Whereas I feel like they would be better served with a surgical procedure.

Jeremy: Which is nice when they go into your center? For instance, if they are going strictly for injectables, there's something else that you see that they can benefit from. You're able to offer that, and they don't have to go anywhere else.

Elliot: Absolutely. When patients come in, I always try to get to the root question of why they are there, and what exactly is the part of their appearance that they are trying to correct. I feel that once I make this diagnosis, then that makes it more straightforward to determine a treatment course. So a patient who comes in and says I want to have injectables, and I ask them why and they explain. I also come to the conclusion that what they want for the injectables can better be treated with surgery. Rather than just saying you come in for injectables, fine I'll give you injectables.

Jeremy: Injectables are a temporary procedure as well.

Elliot: Yes.

Jeremy: Cosmetic procedures are more permanent...

Elliot: Absolutely.

Jeremy: Is there any service or technique that you're offering, that you wish more clients either knew about or took better advantage of?

Elliot: I think the Oxygen facial treatment that we talked about; that's becoming a more common thing. It works well, and we see a big increase in it over the past three months, but I'd like to see that even more. Our aesthetician also added micro needling on to the treatment line, and that's something that has a fairly small downtime afterward, and has a pretty good effect. So I'd like to see that increase, patients ask about that more over the next few months.

Jeremy: Who will you consider to be an ideal client, concerning what they're looking to accomplish, when they come for the initial consultation and then how you can achieve that with either a single surgical procedure or a series of treatments?

Elliot: I think the ideal patients are the ones who come in and have a clear idea of what they want and understand what it takes to achieve those results. So when a patient comes in and says, I have these lines on my forehead, and I would like them to be treated. That's very clear to me. I understand exactly what their goal is, and I can give them a good treatment plan, with a high degree of certainty. Along with their expectations are realistic, and they understand the limitations of the treatment, then I think we'll do just fine. The patients who are more difficult are the ones who come in, who don't have any one specific complaint, but just have a vague sense that there's something about one particular area, of their face or their body that they don't like. And it's harder to figure out what exactly they are unhappy with, and consequently, try to figure how to treat it.

Jeremy: Is there anything you'd like us to know about you or your practice. Let me read off your website here. Your website for all these listening is hirschplasticsurgery.com.

Elliot: No. Thank you. Thank you very much for having me.

# HEINZ MIKULKA

*Paule Attar Salon and Spa*

Jeremy Baker My guest today is Heinz Mikulka. Heinz has been the vice-president and treasurer of Paule Attar Salon and Spa since 1988. He is responsible for day-to-day operations of the business. Heinz has held positions as sales manager, general manager, and shareholding director at Porsche/Audi automobile dealerships in Los Angeles, California. From 1966-1969, he was a factory manager at the Cape Town plant of Airflex Pty. S.A., the largest furniture manufacturer in South Africa. He holds a Bachelor of Science degree in industrial engineering from the Technische Hochschule, Vienna, Austria.

Jeremy Baker: Welcome Heinz. What inspired you to get into the Salon/Spa business?

Heinz Mikulka: My hairdresser came up from Beverly Hills to Seattle, and she was my partner with Paule Attar. We opened a little salon in Bellevue. I'm actually in the automobile business. I used to be a general manager for a Porsche dealership in Beverly Hills for 18 years. She had a salon in Beverly Hills. My Porsche dealership was in Beverly Hills. I was her customer. It is easy to make money, way easier than running a car dealership. Our main business is hair color. We do close to a million dollars of that a year, and the haircutting comes second, and facials come third, then comes massages, nails, and so on.

Our business model is geared towards career women who work in the area here. The model is we want to create a one-hour service, a one-hour facial, have the best people we possibly can, but we have no fancy things. We don't put your feet into the water when you come in. We don't put rose petals into stuff. We're geared towards those women who are very time-conscious during the day. They come in and get good service. Of course, everybody gets a good massage like a sports massage or whatever they need. That is created by very experienced people, which are highly compensated. They do a fantastic job. That's how we maintain the price level we charge, and we don't have to go through Groupon, etc.

We have a magnificent management team here. We have two managers and then me. We know how to run a business. We're not saying it's a hair salon and spa. It's a business like Microsoft or Boeing. You make money, and you always try to make a little bit more income than you spend. That's the secret.

Jeremy Baker: What is your biggest challenge now?

Heinz: The biggest challenge is to find well-trained people.

Jeremy Baker: How often do you communicate with your clients?

Heinz: On a daily basis, we have online booking. We have appointment-setting online 24/7. We have confirmation going out through digital voicemail. Everything is in our database here.

We get referrals. The beauty business is mainly referrals. Repeat business, of course, is huge. We're getting a lot of organic customers coming in through AdWords and such things on the internet for our website and everything. We are very active on websites and Ad Words and Instagram, and you'll find us everywhere. We spend a ton of money on that. We do excellent work compressed into a short timeframe at a reasonable price, and that's basically what our business model is for the spa.

Jeremy Baker: What makes your Spa unique from the competition? What do think your clients like most about Paul Attar?

Heinz: Maintaining their skin health. That's basically within a four- to six-week rotation, and that's what our customers look for. They want to come in, and they want to get out. They don't want to hang around here for two hours. We are not a destination spa like a hotel. We're a place where you maintain your skin as you get a haircut, get a facial or get a massage.

Jeremy Baker: Describe your ideal client.

Heinz: They're customers who come to us, have been long-term customers, and they come back. As long as we maintain the same quality of the service, we have the customers coming back.

Jeremy Baker: To what do you attribute your success?

Heinz: One of the main things, of course, we stress is our reception team is a stable team, has been with us many, many years. They know the customers. They know how to handle the customers. They know what to do. They don't have to come and ask a manager or me. They're empowered to do whatever it takes to make the customer happy, and they communicate by internal email to our management team. Most of our practitioners here have been with us for a median of about 14 years. We have no turnover, period.

You want to treat your employees exactly how you want to be treated. I do the same thing for my people. I want to make sure that they are 100% happy. I do anything I can for them. There is support. There's assistance with anything they need. We have 36 women working here. It's a wonderful, wonderful feeling to have loyal people like this.

Jeremy Baker: Anything else you like us to know about Paul Attar?

The only thing I'd like to tell anybody who listens to me or our people in the salon here is that we are specifically concerned about the quality of the service and how the customer is treated to make it comfortable for them to come to us. We want to make it as easy for them. We have to park on the outside, free parking. We make it as easy for our clients to come to us, and we want to get them in and out as they desire. If they want to do it faster, fine. If they want to do it slower, it's fine. We take care of the customer. That's our main thing.

The second thing is we take care of our practitioners, our stylists, our colorists, and our spa people. We take care of them because we want to keep them here. We give them medical, dental, whatever it is they get. They have their parking covered, so we have a good crew of women working here.

Jeremy Baker: Thanks Heinze. It's been great learning more about your Spa.

pauleattar.com/

# HALLE FRIEDMAN

*Robert Andrews Laser & Aesthetics*

Jeremy: My guest today is Halle Friedman, At the age of 18, Halle, Founder and President of Robert Andrews Laser & Aesthetics, entered the United States Air Force, where she proudly served her country for over 20 years in both Active Duty and as a Reservist.

While in the Air Force, Halle became a Computer Operations Instructor, attended college and received her Bachelors of Science in Nursing from University of Southern Mississippi (1995) and became a commissioned officer - thus beginning an exciting and challenging career as an emergency/battlefield nurse.

Halle has worked in some prime leadership positions to include, working directly with the Air Force Surgeon General Staff in Washington D.C., and as a Hospital Nursing Supervisor and RN Manager for the Emergency Department. In Colorado Springs, she was Operations Manager and Manager of Patient Scheduling for Memorial Hospital's Emergency Department.

Halle's extensive medical career also includes certification in Medical Aesthetics from the National Laser Institute in Scottsdale, Arizona. She is proficient in Bio-Identical Hormone Replacement Therapy, Ablative and Non-Ablative Laser Skin Resurfacing; Sclerotherapy; Advanced Botox (Neurotoxins), dermal fillers and more.

In addition to her medical background, Halle holds a degree in Information Systems Technology and an MBA from Colorado Technical University.

Halle's background and life experience are very broad, extensive, and accomplished - and she prides herself on seeing the big picture in life. She remains deeply involved in her profession and has served as the Treasurer, Secretary and Media Chair for the Colorado Emergency Nurses Association.

In October 2013, Halle realized her dream and established the Robert Andrews Laser & Medical Aesthetics Clinic in Colorado Springs, where she is proudly bringing the highest level of science, technology, skill - and genuine care - to her clients. Welcome, Halle.

Halle: Hi, Jeremy, thank you so much for inviting me.

Jeremy: It's great having you. What inspired you to become a spa owner?

Halle: It's actually the aging of our baby boomers and being educated in regards to the science that allows us to age more gracefully, and then having a skill set that would actually be able to be offered to the client. So between all of that, when I started looking at where we're going as far as technology and as far as people living longer, it also goes along with that the longer they live, the better they want to look while they're living longer. So, it interested me, and then I started doing a lot of research and then decided to go to school in this profession as well.

Jeremy: How did you get started?

Halle: I got started initially... I had started researching it and I was actually going to a medical spa and began looking at what was involved in the industry, and applying my background, I realized I was rather interested I perhaps pursuing a career in Aesthetics. I had a critical care background and a lot of hospital management as well. So, when I started researching it and looking at it, there was a lot of revenue, obviously, to be made in the industry, most importantly, my skill set was always to be really precise with needles. In doing so, I decided that it was something I had the background and education to start a practice. Additionally, I decided that it was actually a great way to make, not only a living but make a difference in people's lives. I realized with the proper background and skill set, I should pursue a career in Medical Aesthetics. I finalized that decision when I started going to school in 2013 for medical aesthetics

Jeremy: What do you like most about the work that you're doing now?

Halle: I like the fact that I have clients who are happy every time I see them, with my background being critical care, this wasn't always the case. It's very rewarding to have people very excited and happy about the fact that I can actually make a difference in their appearance but do it in a subtle way with the medical technology that we have...I just get excited about the technology and the outcomes that I give to clients.

Jeremy: What are some of the most popular services that you offer?

Halle: The most popular actually are injectables; we initially thought it would be more on the laser side, but I found that women actually would prefer spending more of their residual income on Botox and different types of fillers to help with the volume loss in their face. However, there are some more aggressive laser services that we do, but definitely, it's the Botox and the fillers that we see more of our recurring patients and clients.

Jeremy: ...Botox is most popular?

Halle: Botox, yeah, without question. And the fillers are becoming very popular as well. There are a variety of different types of fillers that are out on the market now. Fillers (Hyaluronic Acid) are naturally made in our body, it's so subtle that people often decide it's not really taking that much risk anymore, because of the successes that they've had in this industry.

Jeremy: What makes your spa stand out and unique, from others in the area?

Halle: I would say it's just...it's really, when people walk in they feel sort of at home, which is an interesting way to feel, you know, they feel comfortable and not as though they're in the real clinical environment, even though we're very sterile and everything we do is definitely medically sound. It would be our friendly staff, we have very upbeat, friendly staff, everybody has a lot of energy there, and so it's very welcoming and inviting when you walk in the door. That's what our clients have repetitively talked about, that's what they like most about our spa.

Jeremy: That's wonderful. To what do you attribute your success?

Halle: I would attribute a lot of it to... Number one is having the education and background that I get, even when I served. I served in the United States Air Force for 20 years between active duty and reserves, and I got a lot of training in regards to how to run businesses and manage people. The military offers endless opportunities for education, in management, and also in technology, because I have an IT background as well. So I attribute a lot of it to having that strength and experience, but then a lot of has to do with my personality as well. So I believe I'm very knowledgeable in the medical field and, I can educate my clients thoroughly so they're feeling safe and comfortable about getting a procedure done. It's so important that the clients feel safe in the fact that not only do I know what I'm doing, but also they feel safe in my hands. And that makes a big difference when it comes to repeated clients.

Jeremy: What would you say your biggest challenge is right now?

Halle: would say that we've been growing very rapidly and trying to keep up with the growth has been a challenge, just getting all the processes in place, making sure that everything is very medically sound. Further, a person must know the state requirements and ensure that all of my staff has documented training. Just getting all those processes in place, is very tasking and demanding of your time, whenever you start a business. Then, in addition to this, it would just be trying to keep up with staff and finding time to keep up with our clients needs and keep them coming through the doors.

Jeremy:How often do you communicate with your clients via newsletters, social media, texts, etc.?

Halle: We try not to overwhelm them with too many emails, typically we have something going out, at least, every week, with some type of either education on different technologies that are out there, or different services. Our emails do not always have anything to do with our company, rather sometimes it just has to do with the well-being of our client, the way that they can improve their lives and their health, and their appearance, regardless of where they go to get treatments. In addition to this, we're on Facebook, Google, Yelp, Twitter, LinkedIn, etc. We have Facebook updated daily, and we're always putting something out there regarding everyday care for the everyday women. Regarding advertising, we actually have a commercial on TV, print in magazines, radio commercials and also attend a plethora of events to always get our name out to the public.

Jeremy: What are some of the most common mistakes that you see clients making when going to other spas and then coming to see you?

Halle: I would say not knowing the background of their injector. A lot of times people just go on a whim and trust...you know, somebody says "oh I do Botox" and I am potentially a dentist, or even another nurse, that has her own, little room that she might inject in, and a lot of times they don't have the education. I find that that can be one of the biggest, most important things are to continuously educate, whether it be going to classes, and I've done a lot of this, as well as keeping up with new technologies and what new products are on the market. With all products come new risks, and it is necessary for any business owner, no matter what the industry, ensure their clients are fully educated. Your client must fully be educated on the muscles in the face and where you, the practitioner is going to inject... Often times, care providers don't do their due diligence beforehand, and the patient's trust the fact that the person injecting is a nurse, family practice physician or even a dentist and they can just inject anything, this not necessarily the case. A medical practitioner might be able to put a needle in somebody's face, but they don't necessarily put it in the right places, put the right amount in or know the product they are injecting, well enough. At Robert Andrews Medical, I educate continuously about the importance of ongoing training in this industry and in addition to the importance of knowing your anatomy and physiology.

Jeremy: Are there any special services or techniques that you use that you wish more clients knew about or took advantage of?

Halle: I would say probably the micro-needling with the PRP, the stem cell platelet replacement... It stimulates collagen production more "naturally" than other medical aesthetics products and services. My patients love every aspect of this industry, but with a lot of patients, the more natural, the better. This is 100% natural, derived right out of the patient's own blood platelets. So, I would like to learn more about this fascinating technology and marrying it to a lot more patient services. By adding it to a filler injection or even laser service, the body's cells are shown to heal faster and produce naturally more collagen and elastin to the body, regardless as to where it is injected.

Jeremy: Can you describe your ideal client regarding what their current situation is and what they're looking to accomplish?

Halle: I would say the ideal client is someone who has taken care of their skin and their health throughout their life. I find it to be more complex when somebody hasn't and then they want to have me fix what they haven't cared for on average, 20 years. An unhealthy lifestyle results in unhealthy skin and fat retention. A person's skin is a reflection of a person's overall health, their years of neglect and abuse of their skin shows, and if it's not in a good place to start working from as a practitioner. Reversing 20 years or more of damage is difficult. The ideal Aesthetics Patient is a person that has already been caring for their bodies, to include their skin. The best outcomes are those who have cared for themselves and continue to do so throughout their lives. Cells constantly reproduce and renew. Healthy cells are what we all desire and this includes caring for the condition of our largest organ, your skin.

Jeremy: is there anything else that you'd like to talk let our readers and our listeners know about you, and your spa?

Halle: Okay, well, I would say, number one – thanks so much again for interviewing me. And in regards to, you the listeners, I would like to emphasize that although a lot of people look at these "aesthetic services" as being vain, I always remind my clients and to the public, (I do a lot of public speaking, to large groups of women). I remind them that ...vanity is part of our human nature" and it's not just part of human nature..., I always make the correlation, when I talk about this industry, "go shave your dog, and see how he behaves, or she behaves." We instinctively have vanity issues, all creatures do, it part of adaptation and "belonging" so our looking our best and wanting to feel our best is instinctual and there is nothing wrong with this. It's actually an acceptable behavior, and it's necessary to us in our interactions with other. It sounds ironic, but, we all are very conscious of what we look like when we're facing other people. We are an aging population. I always remind my professional patient population that it's important to always be competitive and part of where we are at; we don't have to age like our parents. They need to embrace the technology we are afforded; this allows us to age more gracefully and look our best as we age. This is not a vanity issue. This is the reality of people taking better care of themselves, living healthy and working longer. You know, it's okay to love yourself enough to take care of yourself, and that's what I like to all my clients, and they believe me enough, to keep coming back. I love what I do and for anyone considering a field of Aesthetics, first and foremost, love what you do!!

Jeremy Baker: Great advice. Thank you.

robertandrewsmedical.com

# GALIA BALDRIDGE

*Access Wellness Center.*

Jeremy Baker: My guest today is Galia Baldrige. She is the owner of Access Wellness Center. Located in Bellevue Washington. Gaila uses Endermolift, a wand-like device that passes over the skin's surface and emits micro-pulsation waves that gently massage and stimulate the delicate facial skin. Endermolift can be an effective method of facial rejuvenation for patients seeking some of the benefits of a facelift but do not wish to undergo surgery. While a facelift achieves results by eliminating excess skin and tightening the facial muscles, Endermolift™ can give you smoother, younger looking skin using anti-aging cellular stimulation. Endermolift was created by LPG® to firm and tone the skin and significantly reduce the signs of aging. Welcome, Galia.

Galia: Hi, it is nice to be here with you today.

Jeremy Baker: What inspired you to open Access Wellness Center?

Galia: Well I had many jobs that I have done over the years but had always kept in mind to one day open a wellness center to help people. And that thought was at the back of mind for years and years and one day; finally, I was thinking, "Oh Ok let's just do it!". And basically, I wanted to help people with the services for body, mind, and spirit; services that were not available anywhere. So that is what I wanted to do in the beginning. That is how everything started.

Jeremy Baker: I take it you like what you do there?

Galia: Yes

Jeremy Baker: What do you like most about it?

Galia: What I like most about it is that usually I see instant results for people. And people get that wow moment from the services and people are happy, truly happy. The work is very rewarding.

Jeremy Baker: what's your most popular treatment or service you are offering now?

Galia: Right now, during the year we had to be flexible, and we are looking to satisfy people's needs and transfer some services to others. Currently, the most popular are the French treatment and double lift which is a fantastic face lifter treatment for the whole face; double chin removal also scars removal treatment and body shaping.

Jeremy Baker: Can you explain to our listeners and readers about Endermolift because it's such a unique treatment option. I think a little more information would be helpful.

Galia: Yes, of course, I would love to. Endermolift is performed with top-notch technology from France. It is an amazing technology developed for more 25 years already so it's very popular in Europe and everywhere in the world. Basically, what it does is give a very relaxing facelift treatment and Body shaping. As well as scar removal treatment, it can even help with fibromyalgia…It uses no needles or artificial materials and nourishes the skin naturally by increasing the body's natural supply of hyaluronic acid, collagen, and elastin. The results often can be seen immediately, as your skin begins to lift naturally and take on a youthful, healthy glow. Treatments are provided over the course of several months to reach a result plateau. Our patients appreciate their rejuvenated appearance so much that many continue with several each year to look their best.

Jeremy Baker: Interesting. As far as I know you're the only one on the West Coast that has this treatment available. Is that correct?

Galia: Yes definitely Washington State we are the only one with this equipment so far.

Jeremy Baker: What do you attribute your success at Access Wellness Center to? Is it the Endermolift Therapy or is it something else that you attribute your success to?

Galia: Well it's everything together. Great people, great location, great technology, great services and great customers. Everything together contributes to the success.

Jeremy Baker: What would you say your biggest challenge is now?

Galia: The biggest challenge right now is the traffic. Traffic in the Seattle area is the major problem.

Jeremy Baker: I guess that's everybody's challenge right now.

Galia: Yes and it does limit our growth because we would like to open more locations and traffic is something that we are struggling with and our clients too.

Jeremy Baker: How often do you communicate with your clients via Facebook, social media channels, Newsletter, text et cetera.

Galia: We communicate at least twice per month with an email. We let our clients know what is special for the month. We have a large membership, and we also have special promotions for members.

Jeremy Baker: Ok

Galia: So that's per month.

Jeremy Baker: Ok. What are, mistakes that you see your clients make when they come into Access Wellness Center and are coming from other spas?

Galia: The most common are that our clients are hurt from other treatments. Botox injections, lasers and other painful treatments and even liposuction. They come to us to fix them, and that's what we do. We try to fix scars, and we try to do anything possible to help those people who are very disappointed in the other services, and we love what we do.

Jeremy Baker: Are there any services or treatments that you offer there that you wish more clients knew about or took advantage of?

Galia: Yes of course. The Endermolift treatment for a relaxing, non-surgical Facelift, double chin removal, cellulite and fat removal, fibromyalgia treatment, and lymphatic drainage.

Jeremy Baker: Can you describe your ideal client?

Galia: We love our customers. Every client is an ideal client. We are focused on every person's particular and specific needs. Every treatment, from all of our services, is customized to suit best the specific needs of our clients. So we love our clients, and every client is welcomed and seen as an ideal client for us.

Jeremy Baker: Before we end, is there anything else you want our listeners or readers to know about Access Wellness Center?

Galia: Yes Access Wellness Center is a very friendly and upbeat environment, and the atmosphere is nice. When people come to us there it's not really the traditional spa environment but the place is exquisite and clean and friendly, and we have the best equipment in the world. So I encourage whoever is listening or reading this to contact us online at accesswellnesscenter.com. There are videos and other information about our treatments and also just stop by and give us a try, and we offer free consultations and demonstrations because the technology is new and people don't know much about it and in general, you can see us on Facebook and other social media and give us a call at any time at 425-732-4799.

Interview: Alright wonderful Galia. It's been great speaking with you and sharing some excellent information. Thank you for sharing that with our readers and listeners. That will conclude our conversation. Thanks once again and have a great day.

Galia: Thank you very much, Jeremy, thank you.

accesswellnesscenter.com

# RENIA WILLIAMS

*Paradise Nail Lounge*

Jeremy: I have with me today Renia Williams, owner of Paradise Nail Lounge located in Waldorf, Maryland. Paradise Nails is an all-natural nail care lounge with a Caribbean influence, and it provides luxury hand and foot treatments for men and women. With over thirty years' experience in the beauty and hospitality industry, Renia is committed to providing her guests with healthy, eco-friendly and organic products. Guests are pampered in a tranquil setting, designed to rejuvenate that mind, body, and spirit. Welcome, Renia.

Renia: Thank you.

Jeremy: So let's start off by letting our listeners know about your background and how you became a spa owner.

Renia: Ok, I've been in the hospitality industry for almost thirty years, in your more high end, upscale hotels, for example, the Ritz Carlton, the Oriental Mandarin, The Willet Hotel, which is in Washington, all of these are in Washington DC, Virginia area. So working in a spa and having a particular type of clientele, interacting with them and meeting the guests expectations was a great experience for me to do something on my own to offer that same experience but just at less of a less price due mostly to geography...

Jeremy: Are you in a smaller community?

Renia: Yes, I'm not in the downtown area, I'm in a suburban area. More of a family oriented area, which my clients do want who works in the city, so that's not a real bearing on my business at all.

Jeremy: Ok. What do you like most about the work that you're doing now?

Renia: The individuality because I make appointments only, the one on one interaction, a lot of nail salons have ten, twenty chairs lined up, I have a personal relationship so for example, a lot of my guests here are age thirty to eighty-five years old. They may have certain feet issues, in some of the larger feet and nail chair shops, everybody is looking and maybe making little comments, but here you don't have that, and that makes me unique, and I specialize in diabetic clients as well.

Jeremy: That's great. So why don't you let us know some of the most popular services that you're offering now?

Renia: Well the most popular is my signature pedicure, which is a Caribbean influence. We do the exfoliation infused with kiwi, lime and lemon, which is a sugar base and then also my peppermint, waterless pedicure.

Jeremy: That's unique.

Renia: Yes it is, and I'm the only one in this geographic area who offers that, but my clients and guests they love it. It's a different experience.

Jeremy: Can you describe that a bit more in detail?

Renia: Well with the portiless pedicure, the talgon fused with whichever essential scent they choose, it could be grapefruit, it could be Pendergrass it could be peppermint, and the steamed towels are blended with those scents. The client's feet are cleaned first, and then it's softened with, if they need a towel treatment I'm going to put that on, and then it's covered with what feels like a plastic wrapping and then said towel goes over the foot, and now that heat is going to soften the skin which is going to allow me to continue with the foot buffing of the heels and removing of calluses. Then after that I take another warm steam infused towel with some of the foot soaps and really clean down the foot, and then I use exfoliation from the knee down, over the whole foot and then it's wrapped in the steamed towel again, and then I put a dry towel over it, and they sit for about ten minutes and then after that it's followed up with a gentle reflexology foot massage.

Jeremy: That sounds nice. It looks like you have happy clients.

Renia: Yes I do because you're reclined back in the chair the whole time, so that gives you an enjoyable experience because you're not sitting straight up and most of the clients tend to go to sleep at that time as well.

Jeremy: Do you get a lot of repeat business?

Renia: Yes, I would say ninety percent of my clients are regulars, and they have a continuous booking, so before they leave they go ahead and schedule, some have standing appointments that I already know ok, this particular guest will schedule three weeks from now, because that is on my books, so that really helps my business.

Jeremy: You have a fairly extensive background in the spa industry, in the corporate spa industry for that matter, were you able to leverage some of those skills and experiences that you have into your entrepreneurial endeavors?

Renia: Yes, especially with the level of customer service you get when you work with Ritz Carlton, or you're in the Willet Hotel, the service is very high, and the anticipation of your guests of their needs is what they like. So I have a guest that comes to me, and I know that she likes a certain tea, this is in the hotel, so you find out when they come you have that there, and that's a big wow factor, so then when you come to me I apply the same thing, I know a particular client likes a 7UP, I make sure when this client comes I have a 7UP for her and they really appreciate it because it's like oh, you remember what I like so some of those things follow right with me, in the customer service, to my own business.

Jeremy: How do you track who likes what and how do you deliver that personalized level of service?

Renia: Well I have the customer profile cards that they fill out when they come, and it also gives me an insight on whether they have any medical issues, if they're allergic to certain things, so I know not to use a nut product on a particular client if I am aware that she's allergic to hazelnuts, because a lot of products have nuts in them. So I have the profile cards that let me know when their birthday is, their last visit, if there's a particular nail color they really like, I keep a note of that on there so when they come back I can say so, do you want to wear the same color as last time, they say I don't remember I can go back to their card and see what the color was, so that really helps, that's a good tracking.

Jeremy: So just good old fashioned card and writing?

Renia: Yes and then I do have access to the computer to compile that information as well. I have this little file box, and I just go right to it.

Jeremy: A strategy to offer a personalized service, it sounds like it's working great for you and perfect for your clients. This book is all about day spa, med spa success and it looks like you're successful .You've mentioned some things that you feel make you successful. Is there anything else that you would attribute your success to?

Renia: I would say mainly my outgoing personality, the diversity I have within myself. My business is open to any guest, my clients that come to my shop; I call them guests. Anyone that comes to me, because of my personality, it doesn't matter where you come from or what your family background is, anybody is put on this high pedestal no matter what, so I think that's something that stands out about me.

Jeremy: The VIP treatment.

Renia: Yes, and I do have local celebrities that do come to my shop, I'm not at liberty to say names but that's a good asset for me as well, and when some of the clients who are not popular by name when they see that, that makes them feel just as special because I'm treating them the same way, I'm getting the same great experience as the other person had.

Jeremy: What would you say your biggest challenge is right now?

Renia: My biggest challenge I would say now is to educate my clients in, in this industry it's forever evolving, and you have some shops that don't practice good standards, and some that do so I'm constantly educating them and my biggest challenge is keeping up with this industry, what's new, state laws, what should be going on within your business and I'm just making my clients aware of sanitation and things like that because when you do have guests that may have come from, certain spots, and they're not used to the level of service that I have, I open the door for them, I pull your chair out, I ask you if I can get you something, a beverage to drink, they're not used to that, they don't have an environment where children can come, it's a private setting. So the challenge is keeping them educated on this industry, and things that should be used and why I'm using them and what's right for them and I'm always, no one person to me has the same prescription because everybody's hands and feet are different, so I give that person some information and for each individual.

Jeremy: It makes your job easier to have a well-informed client.

Renia: Yes it does, it really, really does.

Jeremy: How often do you communicate with your clients via email, text, social media, etc.?

Renia: Well social media, which is out there, I try to update is as often as I can. I email clients, regular clients are informed if I'm doing a certain promotion or if I'm carrying a new kind of product I want to try on them or if there is a new oil, I want to see how it does, the progress on their particular skin or issues that they've had on their feet, so I send them a personal email on that and when they come in they really appreciate that.

Jeremy: What are some of the most common mistakes that you see your clients making that are coming from other spas, taking similar treatments that you offer?

Renia: The use of the little razor blade on their feet to take care of callouses. I never use anything like that at all on my client's feet, never a razor blade, never anything sharp. The skin builds up a resistance, so you end up with more built up than you had before and then the effects of the skin, it's not getting any better, it gets worse. So when they come to me, I have that challenge, to take care of that, and I'm constantly letting them know that this is not because you are coming to me, anywhere you go, this should not be used on your foot, so that's a challenge.

Jeremy: How do you solve the problem of callouses?

Renia: Well I use a callous softener which is a liquid gel and then also it's applied and it's wrapped and its heat, being towel wrapped to activate it, helps to soften the skin whereas you don't have to do a lot of buffing and getting abrasions on the skin and taking off too much, so it's just with a sand buffer, and then I smooth it, and it comes out fantastic every time.

Jeremy: What technique or procedure are you using now, or service that you're offering now, that you wish more clients knew about or took advantage of

Renia: Well I use a manual foot bowl, I don't' use the jet chairs because there's been a lot of issues and it's been challenging, the Jets hosting excessive skin within those and getting it clean and when you are very busy, in between clients you don't have the time to run and do the proper procedure of running those jets or running those nozzles, put them in the sanitation containers and then going back all the time, you lose a lot of time.. So I use a manual stainless steel foot bowl, and I have several of those, so there's always one, two or three that are all ready to go and if they want, I use hot stones at the bottom of the foot bowl also, which is relaxing to the soles of the feet.

Jeremy: Can you give us a general profile of what you would consider an ideal client to be for you? What they're situation is before they come to you and then how you go about making them feel better and resolving the problem that they had before they came in to see you?

Renia: I would say that an ideal client would be, the client, that when they called and scheduled the appointment that they inform me on a particular challenge that they have with their foot that they let me know about in advance, so I'm already prepared when this client comes, which product that I'm going to have already, and we've already had a brief interview, not an interview but a briefing on what we like to do to take care of you when you get here, that would be the perfect client for me. Someone who lets me know and they're also telling me what they do in between their visits, when they're not coming into the lounge to get their nails done, and they're good listeners, they take in what I'm advising them to take care of in between, what to use and what to do. That would be the ideal client.

Jeremy: Ok, great. So building trust with them and having them informed about what their options are and how you can treat before you even go about it, is that what you are trying to convey?

Renia: Yes, yes, and also if they've had certain products that they've tried before, and they know they didn't get the results that they wanted, that gives me an insight on, I know she said that this wasn't working as well so let's try this on her so, that's really good as well, when you know, when you have that client that can tell you certain brand names that were not successful, what they needed to take care of them.

Jeremy: That's it for the questions I had for you. Before we end, I want to give you another opportunity to share anything else about Paradise Nail Lounge with our listeners that you feel it's important, lhe website is paradisenaillounge.com, and it's been wonderful speaking with you.

Renia: Ok thank you, to my listeners and my potential celebrity guests coming to Paradise Nail Lounge, I would say you will receive a pleasant experience with a holistic touch along with natural products when you come in. You want to be introduced to scents that are going to rejuvenate you, there are no artificial nail services done, you don't have to worry about coming in and being talked to, let's get this, let's get these nails put on, I'm about re-doing your nails and getting them back to the natural state or as close as possible and I will say I would look forward to seeing them.

# TRACY BOLSINGER

*Ravelle Spa*

Jeremy Baker: My guest today is Tracy Bolsinger. Tracy owns and operates Ravelle Spa, a specialized skincare center working to obtain real lasting results through health and wellness, advanced treatments and high-grade ingredients. Her main focus is treating hormonal imbalances along with digestive and food allergy sensitivities. Welcome, Tracy.

Tracy: Well thank you for having me.

Jeremy Baker: You're welcome. I'm interested in learning more about what you are doing specifically around food allergies and sensitivities

Tracy: Well what we are doing is everything that comes out on the skin is caused by something that goes in. So if you are having an issue with food or sensitivities to food, a lot of times we see that come out in a lot of different ways: hyperpigmentation, premature aging, as well as even acne. A lot of dairy issues I see come out as acne. That's one of the most well-known ones that a lot of people know about. So by treating those allergies you can eliminate a lot of those skin issues and then treat the results instead of just putting a mask on.

Jeremy Baker: That's interesting. Are there any other skin conditions that you relate to some common dietary issues?

Tracy: A lot of times I'll see gluten will come out as a lot of congestion in the skin so that one is another big one a lot of people have issues with. But then you get a lot of soy, fish allergies, and things like that. Too much tuna especially if they are not eating wild fish I can see a lot of hyperpigmentation on the forehead and in the cheeks that typically can be confused with melasma issues, but it's not that same melisma pattern that you may have with those kinds of things. So I see a lot of that. And a lot of congestion and things like that in the skin, premature aging and then we are getting into just a food allergy even if it's something simple as it might be. I've got girls that have been allergic to pineapple, things like that. When they eat the pineapple, it causes issues in their skin over long periods of time where a lot of it is premature aging issues, or they are going to get set in lines and wrinkles in their forehead almost looking like dehydration lines on the cheeks. But their hydration level is ok it's just a reaction they are having food issues.

Jeremy Baker: Ok how do you test for that?

Tracy: We have a lab here in town that does all our testing for that and through a doctor. We work with a chiropractor that works with a lot of the natural health benefits, and they run all those through that.

Jeremy Baker: So basically they will sit down for a consultation and then based on that consultation and evaluation, you will suspect certain things and then send it in for testing?

Tracy: Absolutely. We go into a lifestyle with everybody, and we go over eating habits. A lot of people that if it's not a common thing that I am seeing, I have them do a two-week diet diary of every single solitary thing including liquids that goes in their mouth. And then we can circle what the norm is. It never fails. Anytime you have to write down what you are eating, is the time when there was somebody's birthday at the office, or we are going to Rocky's game tonight. Something that you normally would never eat that food until you have to write in down. So I have them circle things that are not normal, but typically most people eat the same foods over and over again because you have those you love. So I'll have them do the diet diary where they can have them write down each of those things and then that way we can see here's the pattern, here's where you are crashing, here's what you are telling me. Let's start first by eliminating these foods and then see how you do. To a point where we can do a simple elimination diet, then we don't have to go through the whole blood testing for allergens and a lot of times that will work.

Jeremy Baker: How did you get started doing this as part of a spa service?

Tracy: It took me almost 7, 8, years before I realized... hey treatments aren't doing it alone. There has got to be something more involved. And just having that natural love for Biology, I started realizing that it took me back to a lot of things that I knew. My mom was a dietician, and there were certain things that would keep coming up that I had to know more so I took a lot of nutrition courses and got a certification in nutrition, so I had a little bit more of a basis here. And then I was learning, and I was like hey this is why these are happening. And it made sense with all the patterns that I was seeing in people's skins and what they were eating, just simple things and this made sense. Eczema has a lot to do with sugar and dairy issues coming through your sweat glands and things like that, and I knew that from my son and it was funny for me to see that hold on all of this stuff your skin is just a trash can for what's not working right in your bodies.

Jeremy Baker: What motivates you? Is it seeing the success that your clients get from dietary changes and seeing the overall health and well-being come through once they engage in a program that you put them on?

Tracy: I love that. I live for that. When I can take somebody's skin and they have just had it, and they have tried every product under the sun and have never had any success, and I can take them from hating who they've loved every day looking in the mirror, which is ultimate. I love that. It is just the best thing ever.

Jeremy Baker: What are some of the most popular services that you are offering now?

Tracy: For single services we work a lot with girls that are dealing with the Polycystic ovarian. So we do a lot to eliminate the issues that they are having. So the oxygen repair is one of our big ones for acne that I say every single acne person has done at least a bazillion times, and then the non-surgical facelift is always popular with my older gals. They do love that one just to kind of lift the muscles back up as well as my girls with TMJ because that helps to relax those muscles not just tighten them and they can get a lot of relief from that jaw issue.

Jeremy Baker: And what are you using for the non-surgical face lift?

Tracy: We do use a micro current for that one.

Jeremy Baker: So obviously your unique approach with the dietary angle is going to make you stand out. Is there anything else you feel that makes you unique and stand out from some of your competitors in the area?

Tracy: Not only do we combine that wellness aspect with it, but we still have that very much a day spa approach. So you still get some nice warm steamed towels. You get the extra pampering services. It's still all about relaxation. It's not a clinical feel where you feel you are at the doctor. You still feel and are at a true spa. You get the nice warm, comfortable beds, all of that and an added benefit of having some great results to work with that.

Jeremy Baker: Do you consider your spa successful?

Tracy: It is, it is, we are actually in our next growth phase, we just moved to our next location, more space and we have been able to add more treatments, now working more with the stress relief.

Seeing how much that stress is causing the immune system to have so many problems which obviously show up on your face and your body in so many ways. So we are very excited we just made that move before Thanksgiving, and it's been fantastic because now we can take that next step to help clients achieve so much more and a better quality of life, not just a great figure:

Jeremy Baker: Wonderful, what is your biggest challenge right now?

Tracy: I think because we are in, Denver. Denver is more progressive than it used to be years ago we are still a little slower with the spa treatments and things like that and getting the word out to people. So I'd say one of the bigger challenges that we have is letting people know that although we have are a spa we do things differently. We are in a different category that doesn't exist out here right now. So people don't understand. If you're having hormone problems, hey we are a spa that can help you with that and help you really get back to more of a natural way of doing things with your body and make it work right and that diet and nutrition really has a huge impact on how your skin's going to look and you're getting that out there and letting people know that you have an option and a natural, healthy way plus a relaxing way it's a very big challenge.

Jeremy Baker: How often do you communicate with your clientele? Facebook, email, text any social media channels et cetera.

Tracy: I do have a full-time social media girl that works with us for that. So we are on Facebook, Twitter, Instagram and LinkedIn, Google Plus and the other one that starts with a P.

Jeremy Baker: Pinterest.

Tracy: Yes sorry. So we are on all of those as well as we do my monthly newsletters for everything generally in the spa plus people who have a special interest in things we do have those emails going out to them about tips and things like that. Say if you came in for a hormone issue here's a tip that we find has helped people in your situation before. We do a lot of that. We also try to keep in contact with a lot of people on the phone usually every other month or so just to make sure that they are not having any more issues of or something new arrives in what they are doing. So we like to keep in contact with our clients.

Jeremy Baker: What are some of the mistakes that you see people making when they come to you for treatments after visiting other Spas for treatments.

Tracy: One thing that I hear a lot of feedback of what people do not like is under-educated staff. They like people to be able to know what's going on and what to do and how to take care of something if something does go on if they can help. They are not just, "I don't know, try this or that". It's just making sure they know what they are talking about and a lot of it, if they get new people, they are not going to know that much I get that. But I think a lot of it falls back on initial schooling. There are just never enough hours to, but they are just not learning enough quality things in school, and when they get into another spa, they are just running through the basics that they have already learned. So that's one of the big things that I see. I think communication with guests is huge. Knowing your clients and knowing what their needs are not just here is the facials we have enjoy. Well, that facial may not be working for that person. You are the professional you need to be able to tell that client here's why I think you should go to this one.

Jeremy Baker: Right perhaps citrus facial is not the best for your skin type.

Tracy: Absolutely yes. And that's what I hear a lot of clients saying they have had problems with in the past.

Jeremy Baker: Is there any technique that you are using now or service that you are offering now that you wish more clients knew about or took advantage of?

Tracy: I think our programs of how we can go beyond just the facial and the all la carte treatments and get them to where they want to go, result wise. So just working with your having menopausal issues, get into a menopause program. Or you're having acne issues let's back it up and see why. What is causing that problem not just let's treat it...Acne is very general and can come from so many things, but we have to treat why it's coming not what is coming out of it.

Jeremy Baker: Ok. Talk to me a little bit about what you would consider to be an ideal client regarding what their situation is, what they are looking to accomplish and how you would go about accomplishing that.

Tracy: An ideal client for us is someone who would be having problems or just know that their skin is just not the way that they want it to be. It could be as minor as that little spec of color probably the size of a freckle on them, but I got to get the mag lamp out to see it. They are not happy with it. I like that kind of clients that they know they want to see something different. They want to see their skin have that healthy glow, just look radiant. Put the aging away as long as possible but in a very natural healthy way, not just throw in some injectables and have plastic surgery. So we are looking for that ideal person that knows that this is going to take some work, and this is the commitment on their part, but they want to put in there, and they are excited to see us and they see that we are not a luxury item, we are a necessity item.

Jeremy Baker: That's a good point. Well, that's it for the questions that I had for you. Before we go, it's your opportunity to explain to the audience anything else that you would like them to know about Ravelle.

Tracy: I would just say: please visit our website. The website is Ravellespa.com.

Tracy: And thank you so much for having us. This has been a joy.

# JEANNE WHITMAN

*Achieve Beautiful Skin*

Jeremy Baker: My guest today is Jeanne Whitman, Jeanne Whitman CCE CME is a Licensed Medical Aesthetician, Laser Specialist and Electrologist.

Her education includes: Health and Beauty Institute, Charron Williams College of Nursing, and Tampa Laser Touch

Jeanne is the founder and chief medical aesthetician of Achieve Beautiful Skin. She has successfully combined her passion for a positive self image and natural health by implementing a non surgical approach that goes beyond a typical facial. A Miami florida native, Jeanne spent 3 years as Captain of the Miami Dolphin's Cheerleading team,which then worked as a personal trainer. She graduated from Charron William Nursing school and raised her two children. Building from her past experiences and education she decided to pursue a career in Medical Skin Care. Jeanne became licensed as a Medical Aesthetician, Laser specialist and Electrologist and began working in the field in 2004.

Jeanne has a genuine concern for her clients' overall health and a passion for her work. In order to maintain an intimate experience Jeanne personally treats each client. Overseen by Dr. Mark Pinsky MDVIP, Jeanne is able to offer premiere medical grade product and equipment. Jeanne creates a custom skin care program including counseling on proper skin care at home. She specializes in unique anti aging treatments including, Rejuvapen, Intense Pulse Light, Dermawave Smartpeel, Ultrasonic Skin rejuvenation and E light Skin tightening.

In addition to serving her clients Jeanne devotes her time to community outreach programs, charities and local business organizations.

Organizations of interest include the American Cancer Society, Serene Harbor, WeVENTURE, Brevard County Fire Rescue, as well as Police Associations and the homeless shelters.

Jeanne's most recent passion is the Bra Recyclers Program. Achieve Beautiful Skin is one of three bra collections sites in the state of Florida and the only one in Brevard County. Gently used or new bra's are collected year round for Bra Recyclers. Bra Recyclers is a textile recycling company. Bra's are distributed around the world through exporters and Bra Recycling Ambassadors to deserving women and girls in transition.

Achieve Beautiful Skin was named Emerging Business of the Year 2014 and a nominee in 2015 by Cocoa Beach Regional Chamber of Commerce Business Resource Council.

Welcome, Jeanne.


Jeanne: Good morning, Thank you so much for having me, I appreciate it.

Jeremy Baker: It's great having you. What inspired you to become a spa owner?

Jeanne: From a very young age, I have always wanted to have my own spa. Early on in my career, I spent three years as a Miami Dolphins Cheerleader. From there I became a Personal Trainer, and nursing school is where I discovered medical skincare. I then became a medical aesthetician and went on to learn more about business. I had taken many different business courses, one of them being from the Florida Institute of Technology. That furthered my desire to build my own business, and that is what got me into the medical skin care field.

Jeremy Baker: Achieve Beautiful Skin is a self-explanatory name. That doesn't leave a whole lot to the imagination. I take it that was the inspiration for the name of the spa?

Jeanne: Yes absolutely. My mind dreams, designs and delivers skin care roadmaps to better the clients that I serve, so those clients feel better about themselves. I feel as though I create safe, inspiring and innovative face maps for my clients. I do have an emotional attachment to them, and I really love making them feel special, and looking their best. So it gives me an extraordinary high when I'm doing something that I dreamed of all my life.

Jeremy Baker: Wonderful.

Jeanne: Achieve Beautiful Skin is just what it says, you achieve beautiful skin. No one else has the cutting-edge, proven and safe technology and the personalized spa-like environment that I have and that makes me unique, and it gets me out of bed every day.

Jeremy Baker: It sounds like you love what you do.

Jeanne: Oh my goodness, I am grateful and feel exceptionally happy at the spa every day.

Jeremy Baker: What do you like most about it if you had to pick one thing? What really inspires you about it?

Jeanne: Helping people to feel special and look their best. I feel as though I create a safe, inspiring and innovative playground for my clients. I have an emotional attachment to them and love making them feel special and look their best. We become friends and I like that.

Jeremy Baker: That's great. I was looking over some information on the website, and I like how you phrased what you do..... really bringing out their natural beauty.

Jeanne: Thank you. All women are beautiful inside and out, but sometimes we need help to get to that place where we truly love what we see in the mirror and to achieve that healthy glow and confidence that we all want.

Jeremy Baker: Because you're not trying to make someone more beautiful, you're simply enhancing what they already have.

Jeanne: That's right, creating and enhancing a more beautiful version of their self.

Jeremy Baker: Love it.

Jeremy Baker: So what are some of the most popular services that you offer, that enhance their natural beauty?

Jeanne: Okay. Well, the biggest one right now is called the EndyMed Radio Frequency Intensive. What that is, is a radio frequency micro-needling device that when used on the face, within a few days collagen starts to reproduce, and it makes your skin and your face begin to look like it's lifted. The scars are gone, wrinkles are just plumped right out, and it looks almost as if you've had a mini facelift, but it's not invasive. It just makes a better you. You look gorgeous. You look handsome.

Jeremy Baker: Micro needling is very popular right now.

Jeanne: Yes it is extremely popular. Right now the EndyMed Radio Frequency Micro needling is state of the art, and the newest FDA approved piece of equipment

Jeremy Baker: Great.

Jeanne: I have used the micro-needling devices that are handheld, and it can leave some people with pinpoint bleeding and unpredictable outcomes. The handheld device's hard to be precise. Every aspect of the computerized, Endymed RF Intensive device is calculated, and bleeding doesn't occur. Other types of micro needling, such as the Rejuvapen or Dermapen, can leave a person with maybe 3 or 4 days down time.

Jeanne: Clients get incredible results with the EndyMed Radio Frequency Intensive device. There's usually only a few hours of downtime.

Jeremy Baker: Okay.

Jeanne: It's a remarkable machine. Another service that I provide is pain-free laser hair removal. It's extremely popular. I have a niche in this county because I am the only medispa that owns an Emvera Diolux machine. It's pain-free, and it's fabulous. It's fast. I can laser a man's back in 10, 15 minutes, from start to finish.

Jeremy Baker: Better than the old fashioned waxing, right?

Jeanne: Oh my goodness yes. Waxing is very painful, and so are the old fashion lasers. The rubber band snap-type feeling that an old fashioned laser sends out along with heat are becoming a thing of the past.

Jeremy Baker: So it doesn't have to be like the 40-year-old virgin?

Jeanne: No, it doesn't, but I appreciated that movie.

Jeremy Baker: So I take it you do have competitors in the area?

Jeanne: Yes.

Jeremy Baker: And what would you say makes your spa unique, and stand out from the other competitors?

Jeanne: There are many things that I would attribute my success to – and that make my medispa truly unique in this community.

1. My location. I am in a high-income part of town in an area called "medical mile," which has an extensive number of medical specialists and doctors. Being part of that environment provides

an automatic comfort factor. We are easy to find and in a reputable area.

2. Our customized, personalized, consistent service. Unlike with other spas, a client will always see me when they come in, so they will have regular care. Additionally, I take the time to put together custom plans for each client, something that typically doesn't happen at larger spas with "one size fits all" treatment menus.

3. Our equipment. We have the latest, cutting-edge technology in the industry, yet we can maintain a low overhead, which keeps our prices low for our clients.

4. Our branding. We are incredibly visible in the community and work hard to be human and approachable via social media and all marketing efforts. And everyone recognizes our bright pink and green branding elements!

Jeremy Baker: I take it that if I was to ask you what you attribute your success to, you would tell me about all of your happy clients?

Jeanne: Yes, I would say all of my happy clients. We probably have about 400 happy clients, 5-star happy, repeat clients. We give them what they ask for, and sometimes we give them more than what they ask for. I ask them to fill out surveys and find out how they heard about us. I also do Website reviews, Google Analytics, social media ads, public engagements and what not. I offer a $99 monthly program that includes two facial services each month. That's taken automatically out of their account, so they don't have to think about it, it simply becomes part of their normal wellness regimen. We also offer a $150 level. So there are platinum, gold and silver levels. So people actually can count on their appointment a month ahead of time, and it's already paid for, so they come. That makes people stick to it to their program.

Jeremy Baker: It's a win, win.

Jeanne: Yeah.

Jeremy Baker: Great. What's you biggest challenge right now?

Jeanne: Relocating. I'm looking to spread out, start offering a lot more and need more room. I want to have a big enough space to where I can have meetings and gatherings where people will come for beauty topic education.

Jeremy Baker: Events.

Jeanne: Events exactly. They'll come for events, and I'll have a PowerPoint presentation about different types of leading-edge treatments. I'd love to have room to do that, and I'd like to have 4 or 5 rooms where I can have a massage therapist, acupuncturist and so on.

Jeremy Baker: Okay. So it's just expansion in general.

Jeanne: Yes

Jeremy Baker: Which means hiring more staff eventually?

Jeanne: Yes I think so. Some of it would include independent contractors. I can also hire a nurse practitioner. I can hire a nurse practitioner at a certain hourly rate, and that person would only come when needed to offer fillers or Botox for example. Also, we've created a wellness program and networking group that offers wellness seminars.

Jeremy Baker: It would be a great way to promote your services, get new clients in the door to see what you have to offer, and let them try it out to get to know more about you.

Jeanne: Exactly.

Jeremy Baker: Great idea.

Jeanne: And about what we do.

Jeremy Baker: So how often do you communicate with your existing clients?

Jeremy Baker: Social media, email, text, etc.

Jeanne: I'm big into the social media. We also send out thank you cards. It's been 45 days I haven't seen you, kind of thing in an email. Or we give them what you call an incentive when they haven't been here in 60 days. We give them incentives even if it's their birthday. Like a free microdermabrasion on your birthday. So we keep in touch with them all the time. We also give them phone calls the day after they have seen us follow up. So we're talking to them, texting, and social media. There are also physical cards that we send out.

Jeremy Baker: Okay good. So when your clients have gone to other spas in the area for non-surgical facial treatments, what, if any, mistakes are you seeing that may have been made at other spas?

Jeanne: The biggest one that stands out to me is they see different technicians each time they go back, so there is no treatment consistency. Number 2, they don't give the education that I do. Most of my clients report back to me and say, you know nobody educate me like you do Jeanne. I would have to say that's really good. That's two of the big things right there. Larger spas also charge more and don't give them personalized attention. With laser hair removal, a lot of these other places burn them. And the before and after pictures, we always do that to show improvement. We have a book when you enter that you can see before and after shots for various treatments so you can get an idea of what you're going to look like.

Jeremy Baker: Good. Is there a service that you are offering now, that you wish more of your clients knew about or took advantage of?

Jeanne: Yes it's the Endy Med Intensive. It's a brand new machine that I have, a piece of equipment. We're just getting the word out. I just purchased it probably six weeks ago, and I want everyone to know that it's pain-free. It delivers radio frequency heat into the skin, down to the bottom layer where the blood flows. And it makes you look incredible. I also want people to know that it's not real expensive. I know a lot of other places that are charging double right now. I have an introductory price of $499. It's usually a $1,000 service at other space, and it lasts.

Jeremy Baker: How many treatments do they need to start seeing some results, one treatment, and ten treatments?

Jeanne: One treatment you'll see results big time. Especially in the lines that start off from your nose and go down to your lip. Those will get shorter. The elasticity of your skin gets tighter, in just one treatment. The wrinkle, crow's feet, anything that's sagging on your skin gets tighter and thicker, and there more bounce to it. So it's lasting and also creates more collagen.

Jeanne: And make you look great.

Jeremy Baker: That's sounds like the latest and greatest.

Jeanne: It is top of the line.

Jeremy Baker: Good. So can you give me an idea of what an ideal client would be for you? Or what your ideal client now is concerning what their situation is, what they're looking to accomplish, and how you go about delivering that?

Jeanne: Okay. Well, my ideal client is anywhere between the ages of 45 and 60 and female. We do serve men, but it's not frequent. Many clients are tennis players and have a lot of exposure to the sun, so I help them to clear up that sun damage. My typical client has disposable income. We are open late, on Saturdays, and even early in the morning to offer business women options around their workday.

Jeremy Baker: Jeanne, It's been wonderful learning more about Achieve Beautiful Skin. Before we end the call here, I want to give you an opportunity to say anything else about Achieve Beautiful Skin that you'd like the readers, and the listeners to know.

Jeanne: Yes. I think it's imperative that when people are looking for a spa or med-spa that they do their research. As I mentioned earlier, there are some larger spas that don't provide the same level of personalized service and care that a smaller medispa does. (Not to mention the prices often being better at a boutique location!). I work very hard to have a positive reputation in my community so that my clients trust me. For example, in 2013 and 2015 I was a top nominee/finalist for the "Business Champion of the Year" Award for the local Chamber of Commerce. I was also named the 2014 "Emerging Business of the Year" from that same Chamber. Having awards like this shows that the community is behind you and that you have proven your ability to be a trusted service provider. We also treat our employees' right, which is important to the long-term success of any business. We provide trips and vacation time for stellar performers, and also ensure that employees have access to the latest professional development offerings so they can provide superior service at all times. We are also a good corporate citizen – providing complementary services to local non-profits. We also provide skin care treatments to children and teen cancer patients free of charge.

I also belong to a group called the weVENTURE League of Extraordinary Women. It is a group of local, high-profile business women whose goal it is to inspire other women to reach their full potential in business. There are a lot of incredibly high-powered women in this group.

Jeremy Baker: Is there a website?

Jeanne: Not for the League, but you can find out more about the weVENTURE organization at www.weventure.org.

Jeremy Baker: Sounds inspirational.

Jeanne: Oh it's fantastic I love this group. It's just so motivational for students and women when we get together. We meet quarterly; however we do have other side meetings. It's a power-packed room, to say the least.

Jeremy Baker: Wonderful okay. Everyone knows that if they are in the Viera Florida area; go to achievebeautifulskin.com to learn more.

Jeanne: Yes. We have all the best medical equipment and unparalleled personalized service.

# JEFF SEERY

*Illuminate Face and Body Bar.*

My guest for this interview is Jeff Seery, co-owner of Illuminate Face and Body Bar. The first location for this Med Spa is opening in Las Vegas early this year 2016. Jeff is an experienced senior executive who develops finances and invests in growth companies in a broad array of industries. His focus is to invest in or start-up businesses that have differentiated products or set of services that also lend themselves to a high level of scalability in a relatively short time frame.

Jeff is currently a Managing Partner of Raven LLC, which houses his investments, financing arrangements, and start-up operations. Current holdings include Wonderland Bakery, Illuminate — Face & Body Bar, Tropical Smoothie and Kayenta Therapy's eLearning Division.

Previously Jeff was Senior Vice President, Corporate Finance Management for Las Vegas Sands, the largest casino operator in the world. His responsibilities included managing the corporate financial organization, and leadership for much of the shared services organization, including Information Technology and Human Resources. After joining the company in 2008, he helped facilitate a $3.1 billion Initial Public Offering in Hong Kong of the company's assets in Macau. Additionally, Jeff oversaw the company's global cost savings initiative which eliminated $550 million in annual expenses and was instrumental in the organizational redesign of the company. And now on to the interview.

Jeremy: Welcome Jeff.

Jeff: Thank you.

Jeremy: It's great to have you. I'm interested in your unique perspective in this industry. Many of the interviews as I mentioned earlier, are more from a practitioner mindset, and you have a different background. So why don't you go into a little bit about how you ended up in the Med Spa Business.

Jeff: Sure. I have a corporate background focused on finance for some years. Moved out of that and started a small private equity firm, focusing on start-up companies and kind of small-medium sized companies that needed some strategic help. Through that process started looking at different industries, and sort of fell in love with the aesthetic wellness space. As an industry that I think is going to take off not that it hasn't already, but really take off over the next 3-5 years. So I started focusing a lot of time on exploring the aesthetic industry and then decided instead of investing in an existing spa, or practices why not start my own and which led me to founding Illuminate.

Jeremy: Okay. So where are you at right now in the process of building this out?

Jeff: We just got our permits yesterday, so our first location should be in Las Vegas. So we start constructing today as it happens. It's probably about 75 days build out to get the doors open. So we're looking late February, to do a soft opening for our first location.

Jeremy: What services are you planning on offering, right out of the gate?

Jeff: So it's focused on three pillars. One is the face, second the body and the third is wellness. So think of Illuminate as not offering the full array of services, that you would at a full dermatology clinic. But it's also not a sort of one trick only that you see in a lot of the medical spas either. So we'll do sort of the greatest hits. Laser facials, non-laser facials, hybrid facials, injectables, micro needling. Then on the body side body contouring. For us I think as somewhat unique in the industry, a real good complementary offering is our wellness service which Vitamin IV therapy. From our standpoint, we're going to have nurses and A's on staff so that they can administer the IVs. But we're thinking about offering to make you beautiful on the outside, as well as helping on the inside are a good pairing. So that's our kind of combination for services that we're going to offer.

Jeremy: Okay. I'm glad you mentioned that because obviously there's going to be competition in the area. These services are becoming more abundant, and offering more of a health and wellness approach is a trend that I've seen in the industry.

Jeff: Yes.

Jeremy: Along that line why don't you talk a little bit about, what your overall brand and strategy is with Illuminate?

Jeff: Sure. Really from a brand standpoint, we're trying to create a lifestyle brand. It's something akin to what Lulu Lemon did in the kind of athletic apparel stage. Or even soul cycle for fitness spin studio.

We're trying to create a brand with a focus on the medical aesthetic space, a brand that offers an emotional connection with our clients regarding both the beauty as well as physical health. So it's fully that combination that I think is somewhat differentiated in the industry, from what I've seen doing my research in space. Where you see a lot of Mom and Pops, and a lot of individual practitioners, but it's focused on just the medical treatment and not the brand of what you're trying to bring to the table.

Jeremy: Do you anticipate a service based on your research this far , that's going to be most popular?

Jeff: What we're trying to do is greatest hits. So we're trying to do things that we think resonate well with our target demographics. But the feedback I'm getting is the fat reduction space. Body contouring is actually huge and only getting bigger. So there's a lot of interest in that. Injectables there's less stigma associated with those, so I think that's becoming more the general population. I think that's a good space. Our differentiator is the wellness area which I look at as the sky is the limit. I mean it's just scratching the surface of what we can do in that space. You think about it from a nutrition standpoint, vitamins. A lot of stuff that we can do to help our clients out, and that's an area I think that we'll adapt and evolve over time as things progress.

Jeremy: Yes it's a massive industry.

Jeff: It really is, if we have 30-40 of these across the country, which is our plan. We can have economies of scale of doing something that's proprietary if you think about fitness and tracking devices. There's a lot of stuff that we can do to integrate that, to bring data to us about our clients, and help them modify diets and over time. So it's really a very exciting space, and it's just the tip of the iceberg right now.

Jeremy: Right. Offering expanded services to your existing clients, and keeping them happy, and wanting more, and now you have customers for life.

Jeff: That's the key. I preach this all the time. It's creating a lifelong relationship with our clients. It is a journey. It's not like a one-time thing. We're not interested in a coupon crowd or anything like that, or just shopping on price. To create that bond with our clients and help them, both from again a beauty standpoint as well as a wellness standpoint.

Jeremy: If you will? Expand a little bit on what your vision is now, on what your ideal client is?

Jeff: Well that's a great question. Because typically from a demographic profile you're looking at women who are probably 35-55 years old, sort of in that age group with some level of affluence or disposable income, doing some of these services. And yes that's definitely one of our focus areas, from a clientele standpoint. But I'm a big believer in 2 other areas. One is millennials. This isn't just about going and fixing from a skin return to this place. We preach preventative treatments as well, so people now are much more knowledgeable concerning proper skin care. So we want to target millennials as well, and get them on a program that helps prevent bad results from a skin standpoint, and a health perspective. That's important, and I think there's a lot of focus on them yet, and indeed coming into disposable income of the last couple years can only get bigger. Then the other is men. Men are, to them I think it's an intimidation factor going into these places. You have such jargons and a wide variety of treatments and stuff, and that's just intimidating for them and not comfortable to go in and ask for those. So that's why I thought it's so important for us to simplify our menu, keep it to the greatest hits and focus on embracing men, just as much as women.

Jeremy: Absolutely .Could very well be an underserved market. At this point, I think the ratio is somewhere around 30% men, 70% women.

Jeff: That's right.

Jeremy: But men have wrinkles. Men have sagging eyelids.

Jeff: That's right. They have all that, and we're focusing a lot on the wives too. We also want spouses to come in. They are just nervous about doing it, but if we can work through them to set up the appointments, make it comfortable for them. Maybe have couples come in that kind of stuff. They're like they want to do it; they're just sitting on the sidelines waiting. We figure we could tap into that as well.

Jeremy: Yeah. Absolutely. If you look at the marketing in general around these types of services, 90% plus that I notice and that I do for my clients are women focused. The images are all females.

Jeff: Right.

Jeremy: But the funny thing to note about that is , like you said, it's probably only 70% women. So having some marketing campaigns out there that are more male oriented could be a very lucrative approach.

Jeff: That's right. And it goes a little further regarding brand as well as the appearance of your space. I mean we are very cognizant that we don't want our brand, and space to be too feminine. It needs to resonate to both sexes. It's not like a sports bar or something like that. But we want to have men comfortable when they look at our logo, look at our website and come to our space. They're like I can spend some money here. I can spend some time here, and really have it resonate both for men and women.

Jeremy: Yeah I think that's smart. What are your biggest challenges now, and the subpart to that? What do you foresee your biggest challenges going forward, once the doors are open?

Jeff: I can spend a lot of time on challenges, and one big challenge is staff. Staff to me is so, so essential that we have to get the right staff hired, both from a technical standpoint as well as what they bring to the table. I can find technically good people from around. But I also want to bring to the table a field from a customer service perspective that you're going to like the Ritz Carlton or a high-end hospitality company from a service standpoint. That combination sometimes is tough to find in this space. So we are very, very selective in regards to interviewing staff. I think my Director of Operations probably has over 2,000 resumes just for aestheticians, alone here in Vegas that she's gone through. But we just want to make sure we got to get the right candidate, so it's taking a lot of time, but that's okay. I rather spend the time up front get those right staff on board and have that customer experience and emotional connection with the client.

Jeremy: Got It.

Jeff: Strong right out of the gate.

Jeremy: Right.

Jeff: I'm a big proponent of not settling because in a lot of cases if you settle, either they leave or we're not happy with them, and you have staff turnover. Staff turnover, in my opinion, is horrifically wrong in this industry, for holding that loyalty from a client's standpoint.

Jeremy: Absolutely. And the other thing that just popped into my mind, because I'm in this industry is how important reviews are going to be. Especially when you're brand new and that first few clients come out of the door, after experiencing services.

Jeff: Exactly that's right.

Jeremy: And what they're going to say online. Those first few reviews are going to be crucial.

Jeff: That's right. Counter-intuitive to some extent, from a profitability standpoint I'd rather over staff to begin with, so have more front desk people, more aesthetician on staff, and then maybe I need to open the door. I want to make sure that people if they have questions, there's always somebody there to answer the questions. Hold their hand make sure they understand the treatments. Be very, very, helpful for them, because that's what helps that experience, right. It helps people walk away; you know what I feel better walking out of the door than I did come in. I'm going to come back to this place. So I'd much rather spend some more money on staff levels as we ramp up because that's going to produce hopefully really positive reviews online. We're basically putting ourselves in the suburbs of Las Vegas for that first one. It's a small community, so everybody knows everybody else. I want word of mouth to be positive. We're one bad Botox experience, and it's not just one negative review. It's exponential regarding the negative press you get.

Jeremy: There's a significant cost to bad reviews, and they stick around for a long time until they get pushed down.

Jeff: That's right.

Jeremy: If you're going to be opening up a neighborhood spa. I'm assuming you're going to be doing postcards to a particular demographic, within the geographic region?

Jeff: To be honest, the jury is out for me on direct mail. Campaign on females, men, social media. I'm a big proponent of social media. I think if you do it well, I think it's a really effective tool, so we're spending a lot of time on that.. Also creating original content through blogs I think that can be helpful.

We don't want to come across as our services, and hey there's special for this or whatever. We want to be helpful to our clients and potential clients, concerning educating them on health and beauty.

Jeremy: Educating consumers on the many different treatments and services available is critical. There are new aesthetic and weight loss treatments available every few months it seems like. Consumers are understandably confused about which treatment is best for them. They certainly are not getting educated by shopping on deal sites.

Jeff: Right.

Jeremy: Those that do run them, and there are many. Have had varying degrees of success with them, even though there's no profit. There are clients occasionally about 1 in 20 or so; that will stick around and be a full priced repeat client. It can happen, but what I've also noticed is that those discounts seekers are going to be the first ones to go online and start a smear campaign. Give a bad review for a bad service, because these spas they get so swamped with all of the calls, and they just simply can't provide the level of service. It ends up costing them more than it's worth.

Jeff: You're right. I can't say enough about how that is not the strategy. On so many levels it's not the right strategy to follow. So it goes against everything from the business model that we're trying to do. We're trying to create a luxury brand, and the last thing I need is to model our business on pricing.

Jeremy: And deep discounts right.

Jeff: A recipe for disaster.

Jeremy: The race to the bottom is never ending.

Jeff: This is business 101. If you're going to be discounting and doing all that kind of stuff, you can always periodically lower prices, or have a special something like that. But if you set the bar so low and you're in that world of hey, I'll give you Botox for $ you can't climb out of that.

Jeremy: Right.

Jeff: I think it's a death spiral for a business model.

Jeremy: I wholeheartedly agree. Is there anything else that you'd like to mention about Illuminate concerning your vision, the brand, where it's opening? I know the website. For all those that are on the call here is illuminatefaceandbodybar.com

Jeff: I'm really looking forward to Las Vegas. We'll have a second location outside of San Diego soon to follow, and then targeting the LA area later in 2016.

Jeremy: Great. It's going to be interesting to follow your success. I have no doubt that you're going to be successful with this. It's a great business. It's a great industry. It's a growing industry as you well know. I look forward to seeing the growth. It's been great talking with you Jeff.

# DR. BENITA STEPHENS

*Ciao Bella Medical Center*

Jeremy: My guest today is Benita Stephens, owner of Ciao Bella Medical Center and Spa located in Newnan, Georgia. Dr. Stephens helps patients shed pounds and gain confidence through customized weight loss programs which can include tailored exercise plans, B12, HCG, and lipotropic injections, appetite suppressants and meal replacements.

Dr. Stephens reviews the patient's history and determines their current state of health with the physical exam and analyzes their body composition.

Since her days as a high school basketball and track star, Dr. Benita Stephens has understood the importance of maintaining a healthy diet and weight. But it wasn't until she was a trained OB-GYN with her own practice that she saw the damaging effects excess weight has on the body. Feeling inclined to help her overweight and obese patients, Dr. Stephens sprung into action calling upon her extensive training in bariatric medicine to establish Ciao Bella Medical Center and Spa.

It was this determination and passion for helping others that gained Dr. Stephens praise from Madame Noire and earned her the 2012 Business Superstar Health and Wellness award and inaugural cover of PYNTK magazine.

Dr. Stephens obtained a Bachelor of Science in Education degree in Exercise and Sports Science from the University of Georgia. And a Doctor of Medicine degree Morehouse School of Medicine. She completed residency training at Atlanta Medical Center and is a Board Certified Fellow of the American Congress of Obstetrics and Gynecologist. She's active in the Newnan Community and a member of various professional and social organizations. Welcome, Dr. Stephens.

Benita Stephens: Thank you.

Jeremy: I'm curious about your motivation for offering types of services kind of outside the traditional realm of OB-GYN. I think it's pretty clear, your motivation for offering medical weight loss solutions after reading the bio. But what about your motivation for offering anti-aging and facial treatments in your practice? Can you tell us a little bit about how you started offering those treatments?

Benita Stephens: Yeah. Absolutely. The funny thing is that when women come to see their OB-GYN, they can tell us everything. So they're talking all about their problems with their menstrual cycle, how much to need to lose weight, how fat they are, or seeing these bags in front of their eyes, and all of those different things. So as I began to listen to my patients and figure out what really matter to them most, I realized that they wanted somewhat of a one-stop-shop where they could come in, tell me everything that's going on, and possibly get those things taken care of for their annual visit that they tend to make once a year.

Jeremy: That makes sense. You've already established a level of trust. And now, they don't have to go anywhere else for those services.

Benita Stephens: Absolutely.

Jeremy: Okay. I take it that you are enjoying what you do.

Benita Stephens: I do. OB-GYN is a fascinating specialty which is one of the primary reasons why I chose it. I like the fast pace of being able to be in the office seeing patients one minute and going to the hospital to deliver a baby the next minute. But I have come to enjoy that part of the practice where I'm able to help patients to lose weight, assist with their aesthetic needs, just some of those different things that they can't get at every OB-GYN office that they may choose.

Jeremy: What are some of the most popular services you're offering now?

Benita Stephens: So right now what seems to be grabbing women's attention is the use of Bio identical Hormone. A lot of women are finding it difficult to manage their menopausal symptoms, or they're having problems with PMS or any of those different things. Probably the most common reason people will come to see me is to see if I can help them with their menopausal symptoms. And as well as they use me kind of associate hormone's somewhat with their ability to lose weight better.

Jeremy: Okay. Great. What do you think makes your spa unique and stand out from some of your competition?

Benita Stephens: Honestly, I think is the fact that is we do try to think outside of the box. There are times of different procedures and services that have traditionally been in offered average OB-GYN office. But when we hear about things that are a little bit out there that could work, that's new and edgy, we take the time to investigate it and see if it will work, and so one of our latest procedures that we've been doing is some of the vaginal rejuvenation procedures with Mona Lisa Touch and ThermiVa.

And we've had great results with those procedures because people are just so excited about having a procedure that's painless, that had no down time, where they can have some rejuvenation, so the vagina can have sexual intercourse without pain and get rid of the dryness. For some of those women, they don't want to use hormones. And these two solutions have been great options for them.

Jeremy: That's great. What would you attribute your success to at this point for the Med Spa?

Benita Stephens: In the medical spa, just networking, getting to know the people in the community, finding out what grabs their attention, what they're interested in, and trying to provide for them. I go to a lot of events. And typically before I was in the practice for myself, I was just like any other OB GYN. You go to work every day. You work your hours, and then you come home and do whatever else. But being in private practice, I've gotten a good sense of what's really important to the community and the patients that come to my office and I think that's helped a lot.

Jeremy: Great. What about challenges? What is your biggest challenge right now?

Benita Stephens: Insurance. I think... because patients want a lot of stuff done and, unfortunately, we're aware of a lot of different things that can help. But a lot of times the insurance companies won't cover it. So it's hard to kind of get patients to see, "Okay. Yes, I take insurance. And you can come for a visit." But by the time you get involved in the actual management plan that will be needed to fix their situation, insurance is probably not going to help you out with that, so trying to get them to understand that, if you want to feel better that you're probably going to have to invest in your personal fund to help that.

Jeremy: Okay. How often do you communicate with your clients? Social media, email, text, etc.

Benita Stephens: Pretty much daily. We're sending out a post on Facebook, on Twitter at least once a day. A lot of times, I'm sending out a few. And we do emails that announce special events and discounts and stuff that we had going and all. I'm a big social media person myself so it's pretty easy to get on, share with my patient something that I found interesting or something that I think could be help for them with their weight loss journey or regarding hormone therapy or something like that.

Jeremy: Do you consider social media an important part of communication?

Benita Stephens: Absolutely. I mean because everybody is on Facebook. And there're all these other different channels that I don't know if the masses are using them. But people go there first. They're looking for the information. They're watching the videos. And so I think you really have to have a presence there if you want to be able to communicate effectively with your patient.

Jeremy: Absolutely. I couldn't agree more. What are mistakes that you see clients making when they go to other spas and to come and see you? What types of mistakes do you see them making?

Benita Stephens: I guess mainly trying to compare that experience to the one that they're going to get at my establishment because they're different. And I do try to customize the plans with them. So a lot of times the same thing that another provider may have done for them won't be what I'll do when they come. It will be similar, but it may be a little bit different. So just, I think, having an open mind about the treatment and seeing the perspective that we have will be an added benefit versus trying to just kind of do it the same way that it has always been done.

Jeremy: Okay. What service are you offering now that you wish more clients knew about or took better advantage of?

Benita Stephens: Oh, that's easy. That would be ThermiVa, which is a vaginal rejuvenation procedure. And it is fantastic. We're so excited about it. For those women who want to improve the laxity of the vagina. If they just want to improve the way the Labia looked. It's just all doing all of those things. And so out of everything they were offering in the practice, that has been one of our top hits, I could say. Women have been pleased with results. And I think more women just need to know about it because it isn't broadcast in the main street like it needs to be.

Jeremy: Tell me about what you would consider being an ideal client for you in your spa and your services?

Benita Stephens: An ideal client will be a woman who is pretty knowledgeable about her body and what she wants, someone who's pretty open to new techniques and technology, and someone who just really wants to feel better. That particular patient, I think, I have the best experiences with because they're usually ready to make that change as opposed to someone who's just looking for regular every day GYN services.

Jeremy: Okay. As opposed to someone that's only looking for a discount?

Benita Stephens: Yes. Absolutely. I don't think patients realize this. Like, they'll spend money on all different types of things, their hair, their nails, purses, trip, all of that. But your health, you can never get back. So you have to invest in it but because of the mentality that we have regarding healthcare and insurance, a lot of patients are just in the mindset that everything is going to be covered by insurance. And it's just isn't. And if you want to have good results, you're going to have to make some investment in your care.

Jeremy: Absolutely. Okay. That's about it for the time that we have. But before we end, what else would you like us to know about Ciao Bella?

Benita Stephens: Well, at Ciao Bella, we aim to meet the patient's' needs from conceptions to maturity. We want to enhance your beauty, your life, and your vitality. And so I hope that patients who are considering coming to us, our practice will be wanting to have those things done and looking forward to having a staff and a provider who wants those same things for them. So we're looking for new patients. We love helping women change their lives. And so check us up and see what we can do.

We're excited about all the different technologies that are out there. All the new things that we can add to patient's' lives and help them feel better. And I think this is just an excellent time to be able to take advantage of the things that are out there.

Jeremy: For those that are listening, your website is?

Benita Stephens: It's www.ciaobellamed.com. And Ciao Bella is C-I-A-O B-E-L-L-A Med, M-E-D.com.

Jeremy: Okay.

Benita Stephens: Ciao Bella means hello beautiful by the way.

# DR. DANIEL LEBOWITZ

*World Wellness Health Institute*

Jeremy Baker: My guest today is Dr. Daniel Lebowitz. He is the founder of World Wellness Health Institute located in Bala Cynwyd, Pennsylvania. Dr. Lebowitz has practiced as a highly-specialized, board-certified diagnostic and interventional radiologist for nearly ten years. He's an expert in evaluating medical imaging to diagnose anatomically based disease. He is also skilled at treating disease through minimally invasive image-guided techniques. Dr. Lebowitz is a leading physician who has learned that, when it comes to reaching optimal health, each person is unique and therefore, pursued specialized training so that he could apply cutting-edge techniques to help patients directly.

Dr. Lebowitz is a diplomat of the American Academy of Anti-Aging Medicine, and he is completing an advanced fellowship in anti-aging and regenerative medicine through the A4M; he is also pursuing a master's degree in metabolic and nutritional medicine at the University of South Florida, that's Morsani College of Medicine. He is receiving additional training and certification in age management medicine through the Age Management Medicine Education Foundation, and he's also trained, and continues to train, with the leaders at the cutting edge of anti-aging medicine, regenerative medicine and aesthetic medicine.

It's an honor to have you with me today, Dr. Lebowitz, welcome.

Dr. Lebowitz: Thanks, it's great to be here.

Jeremy: I'm eager to learn more about your practice, and I have some questions for you about that, but before we get started give us a brief overview of your practice and the services you offer.

Dr. Lebowitz: I consider my specialty to be anti-aging medicine and so, to that end, we're looking to help people fight the aging process in any way that we can. So, we offer a variety of services and treatments for people. One of the most interesting things we're doing is a comprehensive wellness program we do for a lot of people, and it involves, actually, a lot of different aspects of trying to promote optimal wellness. For many people, it includes a component of hormone optimization, and we do that as naturally as possible using bio-identical hormones, and as well we look to minimize the risks of developing chronic diseases of aging. So, we look to minimize people's risk for eventual development of heart attacks, strokes, diabetes, something called metabolic syndrome which is usually on the road to diabetes, and things like Alzheimer's disease. We have excellent ways of testing to look and develop a stratification process for different patients and what their risks are for developing these diseases, and not only that, but we have some cutting-edge natural treatments that we can apply to try and push back those risks and minimize them as much as possible. So that's a big part of what we're doing.

We also are looking for other ways to try and fight back aging and degeneration and degenerative processes. So, when I say that I do regenerative medicine, one of the interesting things we're doing in that regard is something called platelet-rich plasma, and we're also starting to get into stem cell therapy as well. And what these platelet-rich plasma and stem cell therapies do is as they are cellular-based treatments using cells from the patient's blood, or bone marrow or fat tissue; they try to cause rejuvenation and regeneration of the tissue of the body. So we can use these for many different applications, including hair regrowth on the head, facial rejuvenation, improving sexual function and sexual response, and fixing urinary incontinence in men and women. And also some of other things that including treating of chronic or acute muscular cell injuries, arthritis, tendinopathies and other muscular and skeletal conditions.

So there's a lot that can be done, I think, with this regenerative medicine, since it's minimally invasive. It is an exciting path forward for medicine in the future, and I think it's starting to come in on its own, and there's a lot of exciting developments there.

Jeremy: From what I can see, it certainly seems to be a growing field. Are you offering hormone replacement therapy?

Dr. Lebowitz: We are, yes. That is a big part, in many cases, of our comprehensive wellness program I mentioned a couple of minutes ago. That's a big part of it, and, you know, it turns out that hormone replacement therapy is...it's not as straightforward as some people might think. In other words, you have your basic sex hormones, so testosterone, estrogen, progesterone, the little part of the picture, but you've also got other hormones that are coming into play; like the insulin, thyroid hormone, cortisol, your stress hormone, and others. And so, there are a lot of things we have to look at, even juts from a hormonal perspective. We have to try and balance all of these to try and optimize someone's wellness.

Jeremy: I'm curious, what inspired you to get into this field of medicine and open up your own practice?

Dr. Lebowitz: You know, I figured out in my 30s that this was, particularly on the hormone side actually, that this was a form of medicine that can help people and change lives. I saw firsthand, among people who I knew, that were pursuing this kind of treatment, that they were getting results and that it was turning their lives around. So that inspired me to go back and get the training that allowed me to learn a lot of what I'm doing at this point.

Jeremy: So that's how you got started?

Dr. Lebowitz: Yeah, absolutely. I went back, I got training, and you know, subsequently decided to go ahead and make a big investment in making this a part of my practice. And I still practice as a radiologist as well, but I also decided to open this practice and focus on this stuff, because I think, like I said, that trying to be proactive about wellness is where medicine's going, and regenerative medicine and restorative medicine are where it's supposed to be.

Jeremy: What do you like most about what you're doing?

Dr. Lebowitz: Well, I think we're changing lives. I mean, I think we're taking people who...well, I'll just give you an example. Take the guy who's, I don't know, 55 years old, and he's 30 or 40 pounds overweight, and his sexual function's no good, and he's tired all the time, and you know, he's moody, and he's gaining fat on the midsection, he's losing muscle, he's blood pressure's too high... And we can take a guy like that and put him on the right hormone replacement program, put him on the right nutriceutical, put him on the right diet and exercise program, and we can reverse literally all of those things I just described. We take the 30 or 40 pounds off, lower his blood pressure, improve his cholesterol profile, get him having some energy again, improve is sexual function, and it's like a whole different person, and that's something that we can achieve through this type of medicine.

Jeremy: That's fascinating. What are some of the most popular services that you offer now?

Dr. Lebowitz: Well, I kind of mentioned the comprehensive wellness program; a big part of that, like we said, is the hormone replacement therapy. I mentioned and alluded to the platelet-rich plasma, the stem cell therapy that we're starting to do. We also offer some aesthetic medicine, although the rationale there is once we get people feeling their best, you know, they may want to do things to try and look their best as well. So we do some Botox and Juvederm, dermal fillers and also platelet-rich plasma, as I mentioned, can be helpful for some of the aesthetic medicine applications as well.

Jeremy: So you've been growing, I take it, and considering yourself successful at this point?

Dr. Lebowitz: Yeah, well, we've been open for a couple of years, and we've been growing pretty rapidly. We're starting to feel the need to add the staff, and our appointment slots are getting pretty filled up, so yeah, I would certainly say that you know, this is a growing niche, and we're certainly finding our spot within that niche.

Jeremy: Have there been growing pains over the last couple of years?

Dr. Lebowitz: Well, look...I mean, there's always more start-up cost with a true brick and mortar business than you're going to have if, let's say, you just started some Internet company, right? We have to pay rent and things like that. So, you know, there's some growing pains, you have to plan appropriately for capital expenditures and staffing and so forth, so you have to...you know, it's a delicate process that you have to try and get it right. Also, significant expense is our marketing, to fuel the growth. So, you know, there's some growing pains, there are certainly some expenses, but I think it's proving to be well worth it.

Jeremy: What's your biggest challenge right now?

Dr. Lebowitz: Well, I guess like almost any business owner, we want to grow as quickly as we can do responsibly and providing excellent service to people. I think that's a challenge, but it's something that I put a lot of thought into to doing it right, and I think it's a surmountable challenge.

Jeremy: Okay. How often are you communicating with your clients and when I say communicating, I mean, e-mail, text messages, social media channels, etc.?

Dr. Lebowitz: Well the nice thing about what we're doing, especially on the comprehensive wellness programs, is we are offering it as concierge service. And so, anytime a patient feels a desire to reach out to us with a question, a comment, a concern, they are free to do that, and we pride ourselves on having a very quick turnaround time. If we can't talk to them in real time, you know, we'll certainly get back to them within the next business day. And so, I'm talking to patients on our wellness program pretty often. I mean, in the beginning, when you're trying to make all of the changes that you need to optimize somebody's health and wellness, you may be formally scheduling them appointments every month or two, but, you know, they may have questions ever week or two. And so, I'm having a lot of contact applications on that...in that regard.

And regarding social media, you know, we have a pretty active campaign on Facebook and Twitter. At this point, I'm still doing most of it myself and so it's a little bit intermittent – when I have time for it, but I'd say, long story short, we have quite a bit of contact with our patients. I think it's an important part of what we're doing to be in as much communication with patients as possible, to sort of foster the teamwork relationship that we want to have to optimize people's health.

Jeremy: What are some of the mistakes that you see your patients making when they visit other doctors about treating problems that you treat?

Dr. Lebowitz: Well, I don't know if it's exactly a mistake, but I would say that, in my view, most doctors are far too conservative about taking a proactive approach to the health and wellness of their patients. So, in other words, they will say, "Well, you don't have diabetes, and so, therefore, we don't need to do anything, we don't need to give you any treatment or any lifestyle recommendations because you don't have diabetes yet." But it may be the case that the patient is well on their way to having diabetes, and whereas most doctors in the traditional model won't be looking to do anything to try and help that patient avoid diabetes or decrease the risk of ever developing diabetes, I'm much more proactive and much more aggressive in helping people beat back those risks. And so, in other words, when a patient goes to a doctor and doctor tells them, more or less, "you're fine," it's not always the case. We look a lot more deeply into people's health than a traditional practice would, and I think that the much more proactive approach is going to help keep people healthy in the long run. I guess I would say the patient should be taking a very active role in their healthcare and working with people who really want to team up and help them be as well as possible, and not simply just try to treat them once they've developed diseases.

Jeremy: Okay, that makes sense. Next question – is there any service that you're offering now or treatment that you're offering now, that you wish more of your clients knew more about or took better advantage of?

Dr. Lebowitz: I'm glad you asked that because that is a big challenge that we face, at least in the area of the country where I am. We feel that one of the biggest barriers to people being helped by us is that they don't realize how much we could help them. So, in other words, take your basic patient who is going to an appointment with their doctor, and get their physical and lab work and so forth once a year. The doctor tells them they're okay, and they don't realize that they might be able to treat their nagging symptoms that don't necessarily turn into the presence of a disease per se, but are certainly keeping them far from optimal health. That's the challenge, helping people understand how much more proactive they could be about their health by teaming up with the practice like ours.

Jeremy: Can you briefly describe who you would consider to be an ideal client for your practice or your services?

Dr. Lebowitz: Sure. I mean anyone who's interested in looking their best, at almost any age, could certainly benefit from our services.

Also, another group of patients that we can help is people who, as I alluded to a minute ago, have maybe some nagging symptoms, but their doctor tells them they're alright. There may be underlying issues that we could help flush out for people and get to the cause of their symptoms, and get them feeling a lot better. So those, I would say, would be the two main groups that we can help.

Jeremy: Okay, good to know. That's it for the questions that I had, but before we go is there anything else that you would like us to know about your practice, your website is worldwellnesshealth. com, correct?

Dr. Lebowitz: That's correct.

Jeremy: Okay, great. Is there anything else you'd like us to know?

Dr. Lebowitz: I think we've covered a lot of ground and think if people have questions about whether our practice would be good fit for them, they can always reach out and contact us, and we can always either schedule a consult in the office to talk it over, or possibly a brief phone consult just to see whether there might be some opportunities to work together to optimize their health and wellness.

Jeremy: Wonderful. Dr. Lebowitz, it's been an honor and a privilege, thank you for your time today.

# DR. MONICA SIMONS

*Every Woman Wellness*

Jeremy: My guest today is Monica Simons. She is the co-founder of Every Woman Wellness. It's located in New York City. Monica is an MD. So Dr. Simmons has practiced obstetrics and gynecology in the New York City metro areas, since 2001. She is a firm believer in walking the talk. Dr. Simmons is a fitness enthusiast and strives to have a healthy balance in all aspects of her life. She enjoys meeting people of various cultures and has travelled to many exotic places. Dr. Simmons enjoys expanding her knowledge of random facts, and her dream is to be a contestant on Jeopardy one day. Dr. Simmons attended medical school at the State University of New York, Buffalo School of Medicine and completed her obstetrics and gynecology residency at the Mount Sinai School of Medicine, at Queens Hospital center in Jamaica New York. She is a fellow of the American College of Obstetrics and Gynecology. Welcome, Dr. Simmons.

Monica: Thank you for having me.

Jeremy: You're welcome. It's great having you. The first question that I have is really about your motivation. I'm particularly interested in this because your background is as a gynecologist and it seems like you're moving more into the aesthetics realm and I'm curious how that process got started, and what your motivation was for that.

Monica: Well I have to be very honest with you. Working in gynecology or being gynecology as I should say, because we are pretty much considered a primary care provider for women, it's kind of a natural jump over or a fusion of what we do. Because there are many times that we are the primary focus for women. Meaning a lot of young women don't necessarily have an internist or an internal medicine doctor because they don't have major medical problems until they're a lot older. So what ends up happening is we function as not only their primary care doctor, we're also somewhat of a psychiatrist or their counselor. We become a family friend especially if we also do obstetrics. So my partner and I have both done obstetrics and gynecology. I left the field of obstetrics about three years now. So because of that you really have a bond with your patients, and so you end up giving them recommendations for a lot of different things.

And because of that, we figured out very early on that a lot of women do not necessarily feel complete so to speak. There are so many areas of their lives which they are trying to be balanced in, and a lot of those areas they tend to go elsewhere. They tend to share it also with a gynecologist. So we figured well, why don't we try and get everything together and have a place, where they will feel comfortable obviously with their gynecologist hopefully. And they will feel comfortable in that same space, where they can also pamper themselves or seek other services. It doesn't necessarily have to be medical services. So that's where the idea was born for us to have this wellness, okay, but it's not wellness in the traditional term. It is more like what I would call it a Gyn Spa. So when women come in, and they come in for their gynecological visit; however, a lot of them are very surprised when they walk in, and the place functions and looks just like a spa with dim lighting. When I am examining patients, the rooms are set up indeed like a spa room. So it has candles in the room. A lot of times there's aromatherapy, so it helps in the relaxation for I don't want to say a difficult exam, but it's not a top priority for women to come to the gynecology once a year. It's one of those uncomfortable things. So we decided to create an environment where they would feel comfortable, and in that naturally then we started off shooting to aesthetics because these were things that our clients were asking for basically. So we figured why not house it under one roof, so when they come for their exam if they want they can get a massage. They can get a facial. They can get laser treatment. They can also incorporate weight management. There's a wide array of what we have to offer, and keep adding based on what our clients tell us that they are looking for. So that's how we delved into to it and decided to create a place where it would be like a boutique, and a one-stop shopping so to speak for our clients.

Jeremy: Was massage one of the first spa-type service that you offered?

Monica: No, we opened right away with obviously our Gyn practice, and immediately we had the massage therapist. We also had an aesthetician straight away on board.

Monica: And then after that recently we had an Acupuncturist. Now we have added a lot more services. So, at first, we had laser and facials, and now we branch out. Now, we are do waxing as well.

We also have major lipos for those clients who not only want to get a weight management program, but they want to try and accelerate the process. So we also had that when we just opened.

Jeremy: Okay great. So I take it you are enjoying what you're doing?

Monica: Oh yeah we love it. We love it because you know what, there's nothing better than to be in the service industry as we are physicians. There's nothing better than to serve your clients in some way shape or form. That brings us joy because we can offer them a wide array of services, whether they choose to take it or not. But also, with that we also see the transformation with them. So because we are creating a response with our clients. Again a lot of times when women go to a spa, they're generally going for relaxation. Or when they're coming to the gynecologist they tend to be very wound up, and so we have shifted the view of the gynecology office or the practice to make it more.

Jeremy: Comfortable.

Monica: More focused towards the whole woman, not just okay you're coming just for this exam.

Monica: That's very satisfying to us because again, 20 years ago when we started out on this journey of being obstetrician/gynecologist yeah it's still service, but it was and still is taking care of a woman carrying a child. So we always had two clients, or we had one client whether older or younger, but we always took care of them. But in that, we kept hearing the cry for all these other things, and they would go around and look for all these other things, and ask us our opinions. So in that, we figured why we don't just offer to people, who we would trust to care for us. Or to take care of our clients and have them as our staff members, and then again just offer these things to people. That's what makes it so satisfying because everyone who we work with as a team, we respect each other, and we take care of each other.

So it's kind of like we cross service, so we also don't have to go outside. That's what makes it more like its fun, than actual work.

Jeremy: Great. You have the existing client base there, so makes sense. A trusting relationship is formed, and you can offer all those additional services. That's great. Without them having to go anywhere else. What's the most popular med spa service right now that you're offering?

Monica: Depends on the day of the week, to be honest. I mean a lot of our clients enjoy coming in for facials. Facials and I would say laser at this point, just because again it's seasonal. Once summer is over everyone wants to take care of their skin, and so we tend to be busiest the end of September all the way straight through until May. So yes the facial tends to be very busy. Our massage therapist is very busy after the holidays, because everyone seems to want to relax between January and April. So the winter months are superb times. Our acupuncturist she's just busy all the time. She has her clientele that kind of a year round thing depending on the needs of the client. Our weight management, so our lipo, our iLipo all of that tends to be busiest apparently come January. So like this time of the year when people start calling because they want to start getting set for their resolutions. And that usually is booming all the way till June till the summer. Let me think what other offerings we have, because we have so many offers.

Jeremy: I was looking at the website, and I liked the fact that you have the before and after. I take it those are real patient before and after photos?

Monica: Yes.

Jeremy: Yeah. It's great.

Jeremy: It looks like it's a successful program for you.

Monica: Yes. Part of the reason we decided to get the iLIPO is because I'm a big believer that it has to be combined. I mean yes it's simple to get liposuction. The 3 of us had decided from the beginning that we were not interested, in doing that type of surgical procedures for the masses. Because my philosophy is if we do that, and you still don't change your eating habits, or you don't make dietary modifications, or you don't make behavior modifications, then what ends up happening is it just going to sit elsewhere. What I like is it has to be combined with where some exercise regimen, and that's my biggest thing is that if you put in the work, this is going to accelerate all of that fat loss, and you're teaching this. Currently, we bought another machine on top of that, because again there are some clients who just don't want to put in that extra effort, and they may need a quick fix. Because today is Monday, they got invited to some major event on Saturday, and they just need like spot reduction. So we currently have the sculpture which is going to be coming in by the end of this month.

Just in time for again the New Year's resolutions of trying to get in shape, and trying to get off those Christmas pounds or holiday pounds.

Jeremy: I'm sure that's going to continue to be a popular procedure for you moving forward, especially in the coming months.

Monica: Oh yeah.

Jeremy: This interview is all about successful Med Spa Owners. So along those lines what I'd like to know is what you attribute your success to at this stage?

Monica: To be honest I think that our success is based on our outreach to the community. Because my partners and I we all met in the Bronx, at Bronx Lebanon Hospital. We all had this desire to serve the underrepresented community, and from that, that's where this is an offshoot. So we decided you know what, we really would like to have this all-inclusive boutique spa for every woman, considering every woman wants it. It's meant for not only those who have access to disposable income but also those who are there saving and saving because they want a quality product or quality experience.

So while from the outside looking in people may view it as a place where, oh it's upscale. It's not, it's meant for everyone. So we have a lot of our clients from uptown. They have followed us downtown, and they get the same experience as someone, who has that extra disposable income. And everyone gets treated the same because we believe that it should be a place where we want to go. So I think that that's made us so successful, because we tend to be grounded in our community, grounded in our patients, because if they don't trust us then who will.

Monica: I think that that's a quote-unquote secret for success, but I don't even call it a secret for success. I think that we're always humbled by any positive suggestions anybody has. But we're also very humbled also from any suggestions because again we need to hear from every woman we take care of so that we can better serve them. And if we do that well, then we're succeeding. But we never look at it as a success, we look at it as okay this is something which we enjoy doing, and we're going to continue to strive to make it better for our clients.

Jeremy: That's great. What's your biggest challenge now?

Monica: Our biggest challenge to be quite honest is trying to cover everything, because I think soon enough we may have to move, because we're outgrowing our space. Because we keep adding staff as we decided to have different offerings and everything. So we tend to get a little more bustling than we would like. So to try and maintain that calmness, that serenity which we envisioned we may have to branch out. Just because we're getting a little bit bigger.

Jeremy: You need a square footage in New York City, that's not so easy to come by.

Monica: Exactly, exactly. So that's why we try and temporize it as much as we can. Now we started opening weekends because for the last almost three years since we began we've only worked four days a week.

So Monday-Wednesday-Thursday has been dedicated just to the spa, so there are no medical services on those days. And on Friday recently we had to extend to Saturday, and now we may have to extend to Sunday very soon. So that we can accommodate all of these women, who really would like to come in on again their off days, depending on what their lifestyle is like.

Jeremy: How often do you communicate with your clients? Email, social media, I mean text, etc.

Monica: I see. That is very, very peculiar for us, because as we know nowadays many businesses, they thrive with social media. We did not do social media at all. So for the first two years, it was just our client base, which we had through our medical links. So our patients would come in they would see us, then discover that we had all these other services, and it would just be internal. But then as we got bigger and bigger, this year we decided okay this year was going to be the spotlight at our spa, and try and grow it a little bit more on behalf of our patients. Our patients were asking you guys have this, you guys have that. We're like okay you know what let's try and understand that. So with that, that's when we decided that maybe we should also now start to have a presence on social media. So it's only been I'd say in the last 3, four months that we have a presence now on Facebook.

Jeremy: Wow

Monica: On Facebook. Twitter not so much

Jeremy: Better late to the party than never, right?

Monica: Exactly. Again I mean thank goodness we didn't have to do all that because again we naturally had the clientele and so it was just internal. Just word of mouth, and that's how we've grown so exponentially, has been just word of mouth. I've always believed that's the best of the best. However we were brought to see it, okay maybe you guys have a voice and since we are pretty much the only Gym spa. Because it's not just a medi spa, it truly is a spa. Because most medi spas they offer injectable and things like that.

However we truly are like if you just want a facial, or you just want your eyebrows done, we can do that. So it is like a salon, like a spa. So because our model has not penetrated anywhere else in America yet, we were convinced to share this because hopefully other people would be inspired, and they would notice the difference in their clients as well. Because it does make a difference, that whole spa quality, because women come with a different mind frame, coming to a doctor's office. They don't view it as drudgery. They view it as okay I'm going to see Dr. Simmons, and while I'm there, I'll get a massage. It's more like they're looking forward to it; as opposed to when I have to go.

Jeremy: Right I can see that. Do you see any mistakes that your current clients have made, when going to other med spas and getting aesthetic treatments elsewhere?

Monica: Well I can only tell you what they have told me. I mean there are some clients who we have who come in for injectables which yeah, our staff has to try and start from scratch, so to speak which is very difficult. I'm not sure whether you are familiar with injectables, but basically, with injectables you kind of have to wait for it to kind of wear off, to start all over again to re-sculpture whatever part of the body that is. Sometimes that may not be preferable for the client. But again our goal is not just to please the client, but to also do what would be beneficial to them or for them. So yeah I think on that end, those are the areas that we see the most, okay it may not have been the perfect job or the best job. But when they come to us we try and pull up whatever has been done previously.

Jeremy: Is there a service that you're offering now, that you wish more of your clients knew about or took better advantage of?

Monica: I mean right off the top of my head I would tell you that, our newest laser machine is not a laser for women who are looking just for skin rejuvenation, and or laser hair removal. We ended up being inadvertently pioneers on. There's this new machine, not available in America. It has been in Italy for the last seven years, and it's called the Mona Lisa Touch. This machine is revolutionary in the sense that, it mainly is targeted for our older clients. When I say our older clients, I mean, our more mature ones who are like maybe late 30's, 40's, and there's a medical indication for it, and it also has a dual use as I explained it. So many women at their age, there's a lessening of estrogen in their body.

What ends up happening is that their vagina becomes a little dryer, and they start to have urinary symptoms such as incontinence or loss of urine without prying. So what this machine does is help to revert the vagina back to a younger phase. Meaning it brings back the folds as I call it, or the wrinkles. But the one area which women would like to keep wrinkles for the rest of their life would be the vagina not on their face. So what this does is it revert you back to having that lubrication as before. It tightens it, so that's like a second effect. It tightens it because it resurfaces the collagen, and it's great for our clients, who have battled breast cancer, or they're breast cancer survivors, or they have lupus. Some other medical condition which they cannot take estrogen. It has made such a huge impact in a woman's life because the treatments are just three treatments.

They are 4-6 weeks apart so very similar, to when a woman comes in for skin rejuvenation. But after the three treatments, then they just need a touch up once a year which is revolutionary. Because patients who used to suffer in silence with very dry vaginas, and having painful intercourse and all these urinary symptoms. And there was not much we could do to help them; now we do have something. The secondary benefit which comes with that is that because I am a vaginal surgeon, and I specialize in vaginal reconstruction. This offers a lot of, our younger patients as well a non-surgical treatment for a very lax vaginal wall or a little bit of collapse or uterine collapse as we call it. But basically after childbirth a lot of women tend to get a lot of scarring; this will also help to restore it without them having to go under the knife. So that's why it's revolutionary. It so happens when our colleague got the permission from the FDA, to bring the machine here and use it as a study last year and got FDA approval. Then we were approached shortly after that to test the machine and we brought on the spot. So that's our greatest, greatest thing which we do have because there's a medical indication. Also, again it's kind of 2 in one. So medically women can use it for those who truly have an issue but also it can be used as a non-surgical with means of tightening the vagina, and it's a lot less expensive.

Jeremy: Can you describe an ideal client for you right now? And what I mean is basically what their situation is, what they're looking to accomplish? And then how you go about delivering what they need to accomplish?

Monica: Okay. Well, it depends on what they are looking to accomplish. So when you say it like that, I mean the first thing that comes to my mind would be someone who's coming in apparently for their annuals, or they do an exam.

And they're also concerned about unplanned recent weight gain. So what I tend to do what we do, just because we're physicians we first rule out any medical cause. Then once we rule out any medical cause, then we can truly sit down with the client and say, okay your thyroid is fine, your entire hormone is fine, all of your blood work is fine, and everything looks good. So now let's go over your nutrition. Let's go over your diet. Let's go over your average day. Let's go over exercise and then in that way; then I get to come full circle with them. Because again they come in for some other complaints, which happens to be obviously very distressing to the patient, and then we take it from there.

We revamp this higher thinking, and we make it customized to them, and start with some program where they will have a follow up with us. Or follow up with our nutritionist because now I've gotten so busy, it's hard enough for me to devote that amount time with them. So we got another team member who has very similar philosophy as I do, because we do the weight management, and they take them out shopping. And teach them about nutrition from the ground up and then they kind of re-learn everything. So we have group therapies like that, and we have individualized programs. So it just depends on what the person needs. If that person wants to add iLipo, usually I recommend for them to try and do the diet and exercise first. So that their body can get adjusted to it. So usually, I have them do that for the first two weeks. So that they're not feeling okay, you have to rush to do the diet and then do the iLipo and the exercise. That's something that can be very overwhelming, and our goal is to try and make it a lifestyle change, as opposed to a quick fix.

Jeremy: Yeah I can see that.

Monica: So that's our usual client where we start with something medical, cause they're coming in for something else. And then it branches into all these other things, and that's what I think is so great about us, is that we get to see that transformation. Whereas before we would go ahead and send them off to a nutritionist, then the only time we would see them is for the annual visit. As opposed to we get to be involved. So if they come in, to me or meet up with our current nutritionist, who is there. He's also a life coach. They're coming in I'll pop in, and I'll sit down with them for a few minutes, and say hey how's it going. Then get the actual transcript, because I'm working hand in hand with our nutritionist. So, everyone, there is working hand in hand with each other. So we meet every month to go over which of the clients we want to discuss. Do you think that you can help them with this, do you think you can help them with that. So we take a team approach for everyone.

Monica: Everything is all again as I said, it's an on the job training, and I think that is the key to why we enjoy it so much. Because again we never thought we would know so much about the skin. We never thought we would know so much about, well for me weight loss has always been huge because I love to work out. And I've been doing it since I was 18. But we never thought that we would be so into lasers. We know about so many things which as an average gynecologist, you have no right to know that stuff. But we are forced to do it because we want to serve our clients. We want to help them. So instead of sending them out to others, because we don't have the time to go out to others to test them, to test other places. What we do is we bring the people into them. If we don't have anything under our humble little roof, our philosophy is we don't send anybody anywhere unless we've gone to check it out. So we will go ahead and meet with other physicians, or other salons, or dermatologist. Whoever it is we are referring our clients to; we will go and meet with them on their turf and vice versa. So we also know what they do, see how they do it, and feel comfortable.

Jeremy: Is there anything else that you would like us to know about Every Woman Wellness?

Monica: Well I think that you covered it pretty well. I mean you asked me some questions which had me, I had to explain. All I would say is, visit us here in New York City give us a call. Follow us now on Facebook, and we're actually on Facebook and Instagram and Twitter.

Jeremy: Great! Before we go here, if there's anyone in New York City, pay them a visit the website is Everywomanwellness.com. Monica, it has been a pleasure.

# NANCY REAGAN

*Bella Reina Day Spa*

Jeremy Baker: My guest today is Nancy Reagan. Nancy is the owner of Bella Reina Day Spa in Delray Beach, Florida. Nancy Reagan brings a wealth of knowledge through extensive research, science and personal experience. She recommends only those products and programs she knows produce outstanding results. Nancy is a nationally recognized expert in beauty, nutrition, weight loss, skin care and makeup. Nancy has more than 20 years' experience as an esthetician, spa owner, makeup artist, nail professional, and nutrition expert. As the owner of Bella Reina Spa, in Delray Beach, Florida, Nancy is known for going the extra mile to provide the area's finest skin treatments, massages, technologically advanced skincare, cosmetics, and weight loss programs.

Nancy has been published in numerous national and regional publications. Honors and awards include Top 10 Florida Spas, Silent Hero Award, Delray Beach Business Person of the Year, and The South Florida Business Journal's Businesswoman Entrepreneur. Nancy has been on the governing board of the Delray Beach Medical Center and is the past chairwoman of the board of the Delray Beach Chamber of Commerce and the Delray Beach Education Foundation. Welcome, Nancy.

Nancy Reagan: Thank you so much and thanks for having me.

Jeremy Baker: it is good to have you. I have some questions here for you and let's just jump right in. The first question I have is what inspired you to be a spa owner?

Nancy Reagan: You're going to die laughing on this one. I was actually in the financial mortgage world. I securitized mortgage back securities, and that world is a very, very different world. I needed something that I thought was a little bit more calming and serene, so I went to skin care school after having a master's and all that other stuff and said: "I think I want to be an aesthetician." Then I got out of school and tried to find a place at that time that was professional to work and couldn't find anything but salons. That's what started me in the spa world.

Jeremy Baker: That is an interesting switch, I must say. How did you arrive at the spa in Delray Beach?

Nancy Reagan: I lived there, number 1 and you're looking at the per capita income, and you're looking at income levels of clients you want to attract. It had a very high per capita income level. That was a right place to focus on.

Jeremy Baker: What do you like most about what you do?

Nancy Reagan: The clients. I've met people over the years that I would never have known if it wasn't for the spa business. I'm just super passionate about treating the whole body. That has led me to get to know people on a very intimate level, which has over the years, afforded me some fabulous, interesting, dynamic people that have come into our spa and continued to do so.

Jeremy Baker: What are some of the most popular services you offer?

Nancy Reagan: One of them is our lift & glow microdermabrasion facial. It's ultrasonic microdermabrasion. Our Bella body massage comes with a back scrub and aromatherapy and some very nice special touches. Our Bella green tea pedicure. Up and coming is micro-needling, which is becoming super popular.

Jeremy Baker: What do you think makes your spa unique or

extraordinary or stand out from the rest in the area?

Nancy Reagan: We are very much a boutique spa. It's subtle. It's very compact and our real ability to focus, because we don't have all those spa amenities like a pool, or a sauna, our ability to stand out is our one on one with the client and this capacity also allows us because we are a boutique spa. Our services have to be outstanding, and that's where we excel.

Jeremy Baker: That's great. What do you attribute your success to?

Nancy Reagan: Perfection.

Nancy Reagan: I'm very much a perfectionist, and if I don't know how to do something or if something's not working the right way or if we're not getting the good results, then I have to figure it out and figure out why and figure out how to make it work.

Jeremy Baker: What's your biggest challenge right now?

Nancy Reagan: The Biggest challenge is having the team of employees see the same vision as the spa. Part of that goes to training on the different modalities in the spa industry, and I would love to see the aesthetician and the nail techs have longer, more serious education for those modalities because they get out of school, and they don't know what they're doing. That requires our spa in order to retrain, which requires time and it's a hole, and once you get someone trained, you never want to lose them because they're trained the way you want them and they're trained to do a service, and they're educated to understand the whole body versus just going in and doing a facial.

I think more and more it's going to be about looking at the whole person and not just «oh, okay. You're going to have your toes done.» But while looking at your toes, you also have a fungus on your toe. You also have some circulation issues. You also have other things so that makes us unique because we sit there and point out to the client, "You know you might need to see, to know if they believe in alternative medicine, you might need to see your acupuncture or your chiropractor or you might want to see your doctor in reference to the following».

Nancy Reagan: So that would be something to take care of themselves which it's a full circle.

Jeremy Baker: It's' also about client education as well?

Nancy Reagan: Exactly.

Jeremy Baker: So how often do you communicate with your clients, you know, via social media, newsletter, text, etc.?

Nancy Reagan: Social media is not every day. It's every other day. We're very, very big on social media from Facebook, Google Plus, Pinterest, Twitter, everything. The email blast, we try to make them no more than three a month, and that's some education, and then we also have blog posts that range from, that's usually once a week.

Jeremy Baker: What are some of the most common mistakes that you see clients making when going to other spas?

Nancy Reagan: Price.

Jeremy Baker: Determining their service or making their decision solely based on price?

Nancy Reagan: Exactly. Totally based on price and unfortunately, I know everybody's on a budget, at least, some people are. I'm on a budget. Some people are constrained by their budget and they don't have service and then if they go to someplace where the services are done properly, then they'll realize the value. "Oh, if I'd just paid $10 more, I wouldn't have an infection in my toe because I went someplace where they didn't sterilize or use an autoclave for their tools" or "If I had just paid, you know, $10 more, I would have had all the hair removed from the waxing because the place where I went didn't really care that I didn't get all the hair out." I think it's a matter of when the clients are looking; yes they need to read reviews. Yes, they need to pay attention about when they make the decision on price, that's when it's the most harmful to them. They'll go, "Oh, you charge $49 for a pedicure?", and we're like, "Yes, because in other places you're used to paying $29, but it's also a 30-minute pedicure versus an hour pedicure and none of the tools are sterilized or autoclaved, and you're getting two massages."

There's quality in the service if you'll sit back and look at the quality, look at the difference between the two.

Nancy Reagan: The same with massages. You can have spine injuries, especially the massage now. They've seen us for their back facials, and the facial prices have gone down, and you can pay $69 for a facial, or you can pay $130 or more for a facial, and the quality or the product is paramount. We use organic skincare, so it's going to cost a little bit more. That makes a difference in the results that you're getting.

Jeremy Baker: Yes. Are there any services that you offer now that you wish more clients knew about or took advantage of?

Nancy Reagan: I wish more clients would look at about having a slimming infrared body wrap and not so much always for the slimming effects but for the detox effects. If more people detox their bodies on a regular basis, it will help them overcome health issues, whether or not it's a cold, whether or not it's something else going on with their digestive issues. There are so many things that could be prevented if people would just detoxify. It's the same effects as going in a sauna.

Jeremy Baker: Can you describe an ideal spa client for you? Regarding what they're looking to accomplish, what their situation is and how you would deliver.

Nancy Reagan: An ideal spa client comes to us and, I'm just going to use facials for an example, they'll come to use, and they'll say "I've been having trouble with my skin for 3 or 4 years, and I don't know why. I don't know what's happening and every time I go in and I break out after my facial." That is a very typical person that says that and that is something that we sit down, we always do a consultation. A discussion is vital, and I know a lot of places will rush through that part of it. If the person doesn't have a consultation and a plan and know what's going to happen to them, then here's the plan and here's what we can do and here's what we can deliver, then the person can make a logical decision on what they want to do. They can decide "Okay if I do this and this and this, this is going to be my result. If I do this and this and this, I might get a better result, but it's going to cost a little bit more."

They get to evaluate what they are doing, and that is a perfect client who is there, and we know that she or he is going to be coming back to us on a regular basis because they have a plan.

Jeremy Baker: That's great. Before we end, I want to give you an opportunity to explain to our readers a little bit more about your spa or if there's anything else that you'd like to add before we finish up.

Nancy Reagan: I don't know if I have anything like really dramatic to add. I think you've gone through all the questions. I believe that there are some definite high points of making your particular spa outstanding, and I believe that it cannot just be like one thing. It has to be the whole picture, has to be everything.

Jeremy Baker: Taking a more holistic approach?

Nancy Reagan: Right, looking at the whole body not just "oh, I'm just going to look at her face today." Your face is an imprint of your entire body, just like your feet are, just like every part of your body. From massage therapy to facials to feet, you're looking at the whole body all the time.

Jeremy Baker: Okay. Wonderful. Well, it's great information Nancy and it's been nice speaking with you and having you on the show.

bellareinaspa.com

# RACHAEL SCOTT

*Holistic Bodywork*

Jeremy: Today, I'm speaking with Rachael Scott. She is the owner and sole practitioner at Rachael Scott Holistic Bodywork. Rachael is a licensed massage practitioner and holistic bodyworker. She helps people with chronic pain and limited mobility break the pain cycle and reclaim their bodies. Welcome, Rachael.

Rachael: Thanks, Jeremy.

Jeremy: What inspired you to become a sole practitioner, or an owner, of your holistic bodywork practice?

Rachael: Well, I was inspired after working in the massage industry for about a decade. I always worked for other companies, and I just felt creatively stifled, like I was always working for somebody else's dream and vision, and I felt I could do more for my clients if I could explore more of a holistic approach to massage by combining the best of medical practices and spa practices, along with a lot of caring, nurturing support around self-care.

Jeremy: How did you get started?

Rachael: Well, I got started by looking for a place locally where I could set up shop, and then I launched my business while working part-time for another massage office so that I could pay my bills and pay my start-up cost. And I used Amazon Local as a platform to get a word out to the community, and I had a great response right away, I was just, like, packed with customers. I wasn't making any money at first, but I was building relationships and those relationships sustained, and now I've been sailing strong for three years.

Jeremy: I take it that you enjoy your work?

Rachael: I love it. I'm very passionate.

Jeremy: What do you like most about it?

Rachael: I'm very passionate about helping people who have complicated pain issues, and a lot of times I level the stress that goes along with that. Individuals who have lost the ability to form functions that most of us take for granted. You know, many people cannot work because they are in so much pain, and they come to me seeking a safe place where they can relax and talk about their problems, but also a place where they'll find real relief. And, I'm just really passionate about helping people break out of pain and get back to lives that they love.

Jeremy: Do you offer any other services besides pain relief massage?

Rachael: Yeah, I found that you can't divide up massage between a medical approach and a spa approach. You have to combine them both, because, with the spa approach, people are feeling nurtured and cared for, and are having this pampered experience which is deeply healing for them. So, the medical approach is needed because if you don't know the body and know the specific techniques to help a person get out of pain, then it doesn't really matter if you have all those frou-frou stuff. You also have to possess the technique. So I just combine them both and give clients the best of both worlds.

Jeremy: And would you say that's what makes your practice unique?

Rachael: I would say that that's part of it. I think, also, the relationships that I build with clients, they sustain over time, so that even after people have regained their bodies and their lives and felt like they're where they want to be, they keep coming back because they enjoy the sessions, and like to take care of themselves, so it continues to be something nurturing and healing for the rest of their lives.

Jeremy: What do you attribute your success to?

Rachael: I would say my success is due to my amazing clients. They are so passionate about healing themselves, and once they find that, you know, I'm somebody who can work with them and empower them, then they go out into the community, and they start sharing with other people. Then, they send their friends and their family, they meet people in the supermarket and send them to me, so I would say that that's what drives my success, it's that my clients believe in the work.

Jeremy: That's great. What's your biggest challenge right now?

Rachael: My biggest challenge is working with insurance companies. With all of the health care reforms, it's made it that the compensation is so low for massage therapists who take insurance that it's almost become...like it's almost not worth it. It's like minimum wage after you've paid your cost, and they can only see so many people a day without sacrificing quality. I struggle because I do want to be able to accept insurance because I know some people wouldn't be able to afford to see me otherwise, but at the same time, I want to make a living doing what I'm passionate about.

Jeremy: Absolutely. It must be frustrating.

Rachael: Yes, definitely.

Jeremy: How often would you say you communicate with your clients via e-mail, via texts, via social media, etc., on average?

Rachael: Well, I don't use a lot of social media, I find that most of my clients are not on social media that much because they tend to be over the age of 45, but I do print out a newsletter once a month, and have pretty good engagements. The newsletter is just to keep in touch, but also to offer promotions. Sometimes I do seasonal services just for fun. During the summer, I offer a body scrub with a massage, which I thought was fun and not something I offer most of the time.

Jeremy: Do you see your clients, either current or past, making mistakes if they go to other practitioners, other health care practitioners, or getting massage elsewhere?

Rachael: I don't think it's necessarily an issue of mistakes, I think a lot of the problem is that practitioners who work for other people are hampered in their creativity like they have to limit how much time they spend with people, they have to limit what modalities they do, For example, I don't upsell anything, I have one price people pay for my time, and that's it, and anything I do is included in that. Whereas if you go somewhere else, you might start with, like, an essential massage at that one price, but if you add hot stones it increases, or if you add cupping therapy it increases. And so the practitioners might not be able to offer those services because the clients are unwilling to pay the additional price. So I think the mistake is really in that, in just the way that it's structured.

Jeremy: Is there any particular technique that you use that you wish more knew about or took better advantage of?

Rachael: Well, no. I don't think that it's an issue of technique; it's a matter of being present and interested in things and connecting with people. My primary technique is Swedish massage, which is the most common massage. And it feels very nice; it's a very pleasant experience for people. I use other, more advanced bodywork methods as well, but I think people respond to somebody who is connected and caring, & who get them and participates with them in the massage experience, rather than just doing a job.

Jeremy: Can you describe your ideal client?

Rachael: My ideal client is somebody who wants to get better and is willing to do the work, and also just who shows up ready and excited for changes in their life. And then when they leave this office, they want to be healthier, they want to exercise; they want to do whatever it takes for them to get better. My ideal client is somebody who is their own healer and is coming to me for support and their healing.

Jeremy: Great. Is there anything else that you'd like to say about your practice to the readers the listeners out there?

Rachael: Well, the one thing I want people to know is that, even if they've lived with chronic pain for a really long time, and even if they've tried lots of different therapies that haven't worked, that they still can get better, that everybody has something that will help them break through their pain and get to a healthier and happier place. It's just a matter of finding somebody who you can connect with and who can help you get better. It's just a matter of finding the breakthrough catalyst and pushing through. And I just want everybody to know that they shouldn't give up, and they should keep trying and work with somebody who is willing to try new things.

Jeremy: Wonderful. Well, Rachael, it has been a delight speaking with you, and thanks again for coming on this program, and good luck going forward.

Rachael: Thanks so much for having me.

rachaelscottbodywork.com/

# DR. RICHARD KITAEFF

*New Health Medical Center*

Jeremy Baker: My guest today is Dr. Richard Kitaeff. RICHARD KITAEFF, M.A., N.D., Dip.Ac., L.Ac., naturopathic physician and acupuncturist, was the first Westerner to graduate from Meiji University of Oriental Medicine in Osaka, Japan. he was also licensed as an acupuncturist by the government of Japan in 1975 and was a member of the first graduating class of naturopathic physicians from Bastyr University in 1982. He interned at the Osaka Medical College Pain Clinic and the Kyoto Pain Control Institute. Richard Kitaeff's research on acupuncture and endorphins, carried out at the University of Washington School of Medicine and published in the journal Pain, was the first to verify the analgesic effect of acupuncture through objective (EEG) measurement. He is the owner of New Health Medical Center in Edmonds, Washington. Welcome, Richard.

Dr. Kitaeff: Thank you.

Jeremy Baker: What inspired you to open New Health Medical Center?

Dr. Kitaeff: At the time the center started, natural medicine, complementary medicine, was not very widespread or well known in North America, and I believed that it was fulfilling a need. A lot of people are not getting helped by conventional medicine, and there were useful methods available in the tradition of natural medicine that could help a lot of problems that conventional medicine couldn't help.

Jeremy Baker: When you say, "Conventional medicine couldn't

help," can you give us an idea more specifically of what you were able to help with?

Dr. Kitaeff: Sure. All of the chronic conditions like chronic pain and chronic fatigue and certainly also the most difficult and most dangerous health conditions like cancer, heart disease, diabetes. These are being treated using drug medication and some cases with surgery but these methods are more heroic kind of medicine, last resort kind of medicine that often has harmful side-effects and if there is a natural method of treatment using natural remedies or physical treatment without side effects, then always that's a preferable option I think for anyone.

Jeremy Baker: I noticed you are offering some medical aesthetic treatments. Can you tell our readers and listeners more about those treatments that you are offering?

Dr. Kitaeff: Yes. In our clinic, we have a program of cosmetic, non-surgical face lift which involves treating the face and skin with acupuncture and micro current electrical therapy, which are of course non-invasive methods. Very safe practices that activate the natural vitality, natural healing response in the body. Acupuncture is done along wrinkle lines and at major acupuncture points in the face and these very small, thin needles that are barely noticed. They don't cause pain. Acupuncture is known to increase circulation and nerve conduction and has definite healing effects on the skin, and we supplement that, amplify that effect of acupuncture with micro current electrical therapy which is a type of electrical stimulation different from the electrical stimulation used by physical therapists. It's a healing type of current. Very low-level current matching the level of the amperage of currents found in the cells of the body so in this way helps to repair or regenerate damaged cells.

We use that in combination with some collagen cream, applied through the micro current probes so the current drives in the collagen cream to strengthen the tissue, tone the tissue in the face and sometimes people will use the collagen cream at home as part of the program as well. At a certain stage, after getting a series of treatments people can continue to get some good effects for themselves, maintaining the facelift effect through using a small micro current electrical stimulator at home. I can always prescribe that, and that can be employed along with the collagen cream.

Jeremy Baker: Combining acupuncture with micro current. That's a unique approach.

Dr. Kitaeff: I believe it's a good alternative to surgery. It's shown very good results both here and in Europe and Asia, it's been used.

Jeremy Baker: What's the most popular aesthetic procedure right now that you offer?

Dr. Kitaeff: The one I described, the cosmetic facelift certainly is the primary reason that people seek aesthetic treatment in our clinic, but we also offer European style medical detoxification which is certainly also a way to affect the general health and the skin in particular. You could say that just about everyone is toxic to some extent, and this can be measured, tested, but a lot of common symptoms like fatigue and digestive symptoms, skin eruptions, all relate to an internal toxic accumulation so rather than just treat this externally, you can treat the underlying cause which is through internal cleansing or detoxification, and these are methods used in European medical spas and clinics, such as colon hydrotherapy, constitutional hydrotherapy, lymphatic drainage massage, infrared sauna and of course acupuncture used not just in the facial area but throughout the body.

Also, we often do injections of vitamin B12, B complex, Vitamin C, magnesium, so natural factors found in the body but usually deficient because we don't absorb basic nutrients enough from our food.

Jeremy Baker: Sounds very comprehensive.

Dr. Kitaeff: Yeah, we do a lot of things in our clinic.

Jeremy Baker: To what do you attribute your success?

Dr. Kitaeff: Well, I would say, looking for the best methods of treatment from eastern and western natural medicine traditions, to what has worked over time, over hundreds or even thousands of years in the case of traditional Chinese medicine or the Ayurvedic medical tradition of India. Also utilizing methods that are verified by modern research and you know a lot of say, botanical medications, herbal medications and vitamin and mineral nutritional factors have been extensively studied, and the research has been published in mainstream medical journals, so we certainly pay attention to that. We have a full dispensary of natural products, and I'd say they're all based on very good research.

Jeremy Baker: What's your biggest challenge right now?

Dr. Kitaeff: I would say trying to fit into the medical community where our type of medicine is not the predominant establishment's type of medicine so that means that we have to deal with challenges from insurance coverage and just gaining acceptance more and more, although the situation in Washington State where I practice is far better than the rest of the country in terms of insurance coverage and acceptance by the medical community as well as knowledge of the public and acceptance by the public.

Jeremy Baker: How often do you communicate with your clients via social media channels, text message, email, etc?

Dr. Kitaeff: We get a lot of inquiries by email, and I always answer those in detail. We also get many telephone inquiries, and I do answer those personally, and it's not an office person who answers those questions. We do have a Facebook page, and we have a presence on Twitter and a website which has complete information on our services.

Jeremy Baker: What are some of the mistakes that you see clients making when they're coming from other providers ?

Dr. Kitaeff: I'd say when it comes to aesthetics, if people first choose surgical approach cosmetic surgery, there can certainly be unintended consequences from surgery that are long term in their effects and not reversible. I think in the case of any health problem, any area of medicine is supposed to start at the least invasive level and to move to surgery and strong drug medications as a last resort, because of the harmful side-effects of course.

Jeremy Baker: What technique or treatment are you using that you wish more clients knew about and took advantage of?

Dr. Kitaeff: I would say using acupuncture for pain control is certainly something that most people have heard about, but perhaps they don't realize how strongly effective it is. According to research, the effects of acupuncture for chronic pain are comparable to morphine, about the same level of effectiveness without the side-effects. With acupuncture for either an acute pain problem or chronic pain, the effects are immediate usually. People can see a chronic neck or back pain or a headache or joint pain just going away on the spot. It still requires some follow-up, some repetition of treatment to establish the response and make sure it does stay long term but it doesn't require a long indefinite series of treatments. Just usually a few or several but people do see immediate effects with this treatment.

Jeremy Baker: How would you describe an ideal client concerning what their situation is and what they're looking to accomplish and how you can accomplish that for them?

Dr. Kitaeff: Nowadays, there's so much information available on the internet and through other information channels that people can be very well informed about the conditions they have before they seek treatment. Although information on the internet is very often inaccurate and misleading, I think it is good that people try to research on their condition, try to find out something about treatment options before they come to see me. I believe it's valuable for them to look at the information available about various practitioners comparing my background, my experience, and training with other doctors. That is certainly more possible now, more accessible now through the Internet than it used to be. I appreciate patients who have prepared themselves that way for the treatment and the programs available in our clinic.

Jeremy Baker: Is there anything else that you'd like our listeners or readers to know about New Health Medical Center?

Dr. Kitaeff: Just that it is certainly one of the oldest and largest natural medicine centers anywhere that combine all forms of natural medicine, both eastern and western traditions of natural medicine. We have special programs in areas that we've discussed today, such as the non-surgical cosmetic facelift and internal cleansing or detoxification, pain management, but we also have an immune support program for cancer support and hormone balancing strategies and using various methods of natural medicine that have a long tradition and basis in modern research as well.

Jeremy Baker: Thank you so much for your time and, that will conclude our interview, and I hope you have a wonderful day.

Dr. Kitaeff: Thank you for having me.

newhealthmed.com

# SYLVIA SILVESTRI

*Beverly Hills RN*

Jeremy Baker: My guest today is Sylvia Silvestri RN. Sylvia is a highly skilled and licensed plastic surgery nurse, with over 20 years' experience in the medical aesthetic field. From the scalpel to the needed she will tell you what you should know, and the best sources for those services. Sylvia knew she would become a nurse from an early age. She was accepted into the RN program at Loma Linda Medical Center, one of the top hospitals in the country for pediatric cardiac surgery and heart transplants. Sylvia has trained in the plastic and reconstructive field in Beverly Hills, California, one of the best places for the specialty in the US.

Sylvia has also been in the busiest and most exclusive operating rooms and facilities, from hospital settings such as Cedars Sinai Medical Center, private specialty practices, and operating rooms. The physicians she works alongside have been featured on Dr. 90210, E! Entertainment, MTV, VH1 and the Swan. Her mission is to share her years of experience and in-depth knowledge, about the exciting array of aesthetic and self-improvement options offered today. Patients can make informed decisions, and understand what to expect, and be totally prepared. Sylvia also started her own consulting company, connecting patients to surgeons. Sylvia is a member of the American Society of Plastic and Reconstructive Surgical Nurses. She has been a national trainer for Allergan, National Laser Institute, Aesthetic TV, and currently, The Vampire Facelift. Sylvia has over 20 years' experience in facial aesthetics administering Botox, Restylane, Juvederm, Radiesse, Platelet Rich Plasma, and Micro-needling. Sylvia also trains physicians and nurses in the art of facial injectables, and teaches courses in Beverly Hills and internationally. Welcome Sylvia, it's an honor and privilege to have you on the show today.

Sylvia: Thank you very much and thank you for having me and it's an honor to be participating in your event today.

Jeremy Baker: I'm excited to have you as well. I would like to know more about the consulting part of your business. And what your inspiration was for offering consulting services, to other industry professionals. Can you tell us a little bit about that?

Sylvia: Yes. I was a registered nurse working in surgery and administering facial injectables and running different plastic surgery practices in Beverly Hills for 20 years. In the 90's, when the internet started taking off, the marketing started taking off. The doctors, of course, started doing websites and more social media, and I realized that there weren't any nurses that had social media presence. The patients at times I would see come in, and they had gone to somebody else or out of the country, had surgery that didn't turn out maybe how they wanted it to turn out. So there was a lot of revisionary surgery. A lot of patients going to doctors who weren't board certified in the specialty that they were looking for, but people didn't understand. I think now people are more internet savvy.

Back then and even now, people didn't know the difference between a board certified plastic surgeon and a general surgeon, or an OBGYN. So I just started a little website called Beverlyhillsrn. com and a blog, and just kind of giving advice to patients on how to find your surgeon, how to prepare for surgery, what to ask your doctor when you go in for a consultation, how to take care of yourself afterwards, what's trending in Beverly Hills. My little blog kind of took off and I started doing facial injectables training classes. I worked at a lot of med spas and started training a lot of doctors, and nurses and nurse practitioners who owned the med spas. So now what I've kind of evolved into is I travel all over the United States and Canada. I teach how to do certain procedures facial injectables, Botox, Juvederm, Platelet Rich Plasma, Vampire facelift, Micro needling. I consult with them and evaluate their practice, give them tips I've seen work in different places, and it works out well. And everybody learns something. I love going because I learn new things too, and get to connect with all different types of people.

Jeremy Baker: So you saw an education gap between the patients and what services were available, and what type of services they should be utilizing, and then filled that gap?

Sylvia: Right, right because there weren't many other registered nurses doing that. Patients sometimes are more comfortable talking to the nurse, than they are with a doctor. A lot of people still have white coat syndrome.

Jeremy Baker: What do you like most about the work you're doing?

Sylvia: I love teaching, and love helping people, and helping them have a more productive office or spa. I give them marketing tips, and watch them on social media take those tools, and grow their practice, or grow their spa. It's rewarding and fun. I just love what I do.

Jeremy Baker: That's great. I like consulting as well. What is the most popular Non-Surgical Aesthetic treatment you see your Med Spa clients offering?

Sylvia: I can tell you that one of the most popular things now is Micro needling or Collagen Induction Therapy.

Micro needling is a process where tiny needles are used that punctures the skin and stimulates collagen production. I would say that that one over the last couple of years has gotten really popular, and sometimes can replace the laser. You can do it on any skin type, and you don't have to worry about burning anybody, and there are not a lot of downtimes. You get a great result, and you can do it on men and women, and men seem to embrace the idea.

They don't feel it is kind of like too much of a procedure for them.

Jeremy Baker: What would you say the percentages that are taking advantage of some of these cosmetic treatments, men versus women?

Sylvia: It's still mainly women, but the percentage of the men has definitely gone up. Over the last few years, I would say it's probably about, between 10 and 20% of men but it used to be much less than that!

Jeremy Baker: Well it's becoming more prevalent. More information about it, readily available, in the marketplace.

Sylvia: Men want to look good too, and they have job competition, they are dating, etc. They have their wives or girlfriends telling them they should do things. The wives or girlfriends will bring them in. But for the most part, the men they get Botox, and they do some peels, and they'll do the Micro needling. They do get light peels, and some of them end up requesting liposuction or eyelid surgery.

Jeremy Baker: What's your biggest challenge right now?

Sylvia: I don't think there is a challenge. Everyone that I consult with is happy, and the only thing that I would say is I would like more people to know about what I do. I do a lot of my own social media and marketing, which is what I also teach the people that I train. That's a big part of it. But it hasn't been a huge challenge.

Jeremy Baker: I'm curious what your take is on some of the discount operations out there. Or for that matter just general mistakes, that you see clients making when going to these spas for aesthetic services? What are some of the biggest mistakes you see?

Sylvia: Things like Groupon can be not always the greatest decision. Sometimes clients will go on there and because Botox is cheap, or the filler is cheap. They'll go in and get their $8 Botox. Sometimes it doesn't always lead to a loyal doctor- patient, nurse -patient relationship. I would say find a nurse injector or find a physician that you like, and stay with that person, rather than bounce around. Because that's when patients start having problems when they go to a new person just because it's cheap... you get what you pay for. That would be my biggest piece of advice for clients. Try to be loyal and get better treatment, and people will know you and you know them, and you will be satisfied with your outcome.

Jeremy Baker: There's such a vast array of aesthetic procedures, available on the market and its growing. It seems like it grows every month.

Sylvia: Yes.

Jeremy Baker: And it can be confusing for consumers. Do you think there's anything that's on the market now, that you would consider an under-utilized aesthetic procedure that you think more clients could take better advantage of?

Sylvia: I would say we all have done a lot of laser hair removal, and everybody advertises for that. Cool sculpting has a huge PR media push behind them, and they have media and billboards everywhere. Since I started working with Platelet Rich Plasma, I've learned a lot about it. PRP is an all-natural substance from your body. It's very popular in Europe and Asia. The USA was a little bit behind on the bandwagon. It's just gotten popular in the last couple years. But PRP is a great tool used for facial volumization, as well as hair rejuvenation, and under eye rejuvenation. It has a lot of different indications. Many orthopedic surgeons use it in the joints, to grow collagen and tissue. We're just now taking it a step further, and using it in aesthetics, and it has really fantastic results. A lot of people still don't know what it is.

Jeremy Baker: Getting the word out about these services is a process.

Sylvia: It is, and it's all about marketing and letting patients know about the latest technologies!

Jeremy Baker: It's big business.

Sylvia: Absolutely, and growing.

Jeremy Baker: Can you walk me through a process of a typical client? A problem that they had, that you helped them with?

Sylvia: I think that communicating with your patients is crucial and especially med spas. They're busy, and patients come in and out. I think sometimes patients feel like that they didn't get the attention they deserved. Or they have a question, and they don't get the full attention maybe after the procedure. So I think that your follow up and calling them the next day, or texting them the next day to see how they are doing if they have problem or concern. It may not be a big deal, but establishing relationships with your patients and just letting them know you care, can sometimes prevent a small something from turning into a giant mountain. Even if it's a small little tiny thing that maybe they have a bruise. If they feel like they're taken care of, the patients are going to be much happier. That and letting patients know they're offering any new treatments. I always tell my clients to make sure you're doing Facebook, Twitter, and Instagram. Instagram is one of the most powerful marketing tools. I have many new connections on Instagram from all over the world, and some people still don't have it. So I always try to stress to them, you have to set up an Instagram account. Let them know you're out there. Take some pictures, upload them, it takes 2 seconds. Social media these days is really important to do. Some people like snap chat, short little videos. A lot of the plastic surgeons I know a doing that. Those types of things just to let the clients know they're offering these things, or if you're having a special, are super important these days.

Jeremy Baker: Great advice. I tell my clients the same thing. Instagram has grown, it's owned by Facebook. Once it became owned by Facebook, it's so much easier now to make new connections and advertise on it. It's a great way to communicate using images, which is important in the aesthetics industry. Before we go because we do have a couple of minutes left, is there anything else that you feel like we didn't cover in this interview, that you would like to explain a bit more about, regarding how you helped your clients or general information in the industry?

Sylvia: I would just say to clients going to ANY new office... make sure that when you go, if it's a new place that the person injecting you, is a licensed practitioner and that they know what they're doing. Ask them questions. Ask them who trained them. Make sure if there is a doctor in the premises, or face time with your doctor if it's your first visit, if it's a nurse or a nurse practitioner. Just make sure you're comfortable with the person doing your treatment. If you have a need for anything, for any procedure, if you're having surgery or Botox or whatever. If you don't feel comfortable, and you're not comfortable in the place you're in, don't do it. Leave and go somewhere else. It's really important to trust your gut intuition for whatever procedure you want to have done.

Jeremy Baker: Great advice. For all those by the way, for all those that are listening, or reading this, that would be interested in talking further with Sylvia. What's the best way to get in touch with you?

Sylvia: Sure. The best two ways are emailing me at Sylvia@beverlyhillrn.com. Or you can call or text 424-274-1024. You can also find me on social media. I'm on Instagram, Facebook, Twitter, and LinkedIn under Beverly Hills RN.

Jeremy Baker: Once again Sylvia it's been great talking with you and it's fascinating. I'm always interested in learning more about this growing industry, especially from those that have been in it as long as you have. So once again thank you very much for your time, and informing me and our audience about your depth of experience.

Sylvia: Thank you for having me.

# TIFFANY AMOROSINO

*Bella Sante Day Spa*

Jeremy Baker: My guest today is Tiffany Amorosino. Tiffany is the founder and president of Bella Sante Day Spa | Med Spa, located in Boston MA. Bella Santé CEO & Co-Founder, Tiffany, graduated from Boston University 1993 before she began consulting for the Lyons Group, a Boston-based restaurant and nightlife hospitality group. At a young age, Tiffany realized her passion for beauty and wellness and knew that ultimately she wanted to be in the beauty industry where she could help others. After reading a newspaper ad, Tiffany reached out to future business partner John Groman 20 years ago, in 1996, who had started a skin care clinic and opened a small spa in Lexington which would grow to become Bella Santé's first location, a day and med spa specializing in blissful relaxation-based and result-based skincare and body care treatments. In the mid-1990s, not all luxury hotels had day spas, so Groman and Amorosino found the need for a place where out-of-towners could go to relax and indulge in spa services. In 1998, space became available on the prestigious Newbury St. in Boston, which is where Amorosino established Bella Sante's second location followed by a third location in Wellesley.

Over the last 20 years, Bella Santé has become an award-winning day and med spa, employing nearly 200 health and wellness professionals. Tiffany, who oversees operations and research, brought on Dr. William Numa in 2015, a board, certified facial plastic surgeon to monitor all of Bella Sante's medical treatments.

Tiffany works daily with the spa's management team, Sara Lahey, VP of Operations and Spa Directors. Tiffany also spends the majority of her time researching new skincare lines and equipment that will benefit the clientele.

Welcome, Tiffany.

Tiffany: Thank you. Thanks for having me.

Jeremy Baker: What inspired you to become a spa owner?

Tiffany: I guess it's going on 20 years ago now, and I met my now partner, the co-founder and chairman of our company. He had started in the spa business, and I was just getting into the industry, and trying to learn the business of beauty in general. We were a great team on the Lexington opening, and it inspired us to continue to work together. I guess, maybe, I'm kind of a spa junkie or beauty junkie in general and between him and me we were able to make a go of it.

Jeremy Baker: You've been at this over 20 years?

Tiffany: 20 years now and going to 21 years.

Jeremy Baker: I take it you like what you do?

Tiffany: I love what I do. I would say one of the most inspiring things about what we do is making men and women feel good about themselves. We take people into our environment and put them out as happier people in the universe, and that makes you feel really good to do that kind of work. I always say, if you take time for yourself, you are a better person to those around you.

Jeremy Baker: That's great. What are some of the most popular services that you offer now?

Tiffany: Massage is one of the most popular services that we offer right now. I think it's because people are moving away from human touch so often in their lives, they're coming back towards it in the spa environment, and it's safe and nurturing. One of our most popular beauty treatments right now is the HydraFacial. It's simply an excellent treatment with wonderful results and it's not a long-term commitment. You look good very quickly after about a 30 or

45-minute treatment. It sells itself. There's also no downtime to the treatment. You can walk out of the spa and get on with your day.

Jeremy Baker: In one treatment?

Tiffany: Yeah. We recommend treating your skin to a HyrdaFacial every two months to see the best long term results.It just makes your skin look beautiful. You'll leave glowing, and it's just a wonderful way to give yourself a pick-me-up without spending too much time at the spa.

Jeremy Baker:Okay, that's great. What would you say makes your spa unique or stand out from some of your competitors?

Tiffany: One of the things that we do very well is to train our staff. We invest in a lot of long term training for the staff, so when you come in to see one of our spa therapists, you're seeing someone who's spent many, many years becoming acquainted with and educated about skin care or massage. It's a reassuring feeling that you can come into our environment and know that you're in a safe, nurturing environment with that type of technician. I would also say something that sets our business in general apart is our standards of cleanliness and our relationships that we have with our guests. We take it pretty seriously. I guess I would say the simple little things that you do for a guest in your environment can make you stand out. For example, our estheticians will email guests with personal with a personal follow up checking up on their skin and routine.

Jeremy Baker: To what do you attribute your success?

Tiffany: Hard work. Nothing is in place of hard work, but I would say the success in the spa environment here in Boston is attributed to longevity and trust. In this environment, in this market, we just have not broken that trust over, it's been two decades now, and we, I would say, in general, we are pretty much the spa brand of New England. We have three stores in this area, and I believe we're well known and well respected.

Jeremy Baker: What is your biggest challenge right now?

Tiffany: One of my biggest challenges right now is mentoring leaders below me. As a leader in our environment, it's really difficult to let go of responsibility and to mentor leadership below you. One of the things that we're doing right now, with a lot of success, but also with a lot of trial and tribulation, is to train young leaders below us so that they can grow and take responsibility for the future of the spa.

Jeremy Baker: How often do you communicate with your clients via newsletter, social media, text, etc.?

Tiffany: Every day, multiple times a day. We communicate with them via email almost every day. We are following up with treatments, communicating about appointments, backroom stuff and then we're always promoting on Instagram, Twitter, and Facebook many times a day.

Jeremy Baker: What are some of the most common mistakes that you see clients making when going to other spas and then coming to your spa?

Tiffany: Well, you hear a lot about things like Massage Envy. Why should I go to your spa and pay $100 for a massage versus going to Massage Envy and paying $39 for a massage? I would say when answering that type of question, you do get what you pay for. In our environment, you're getting extremely seasoned therapists that care about everything concerning the body and how it works and can give you some relatively amazing, but sometimes quite straightforward advice, which you're getting when you go somewhere else a lot of the time, especially the lower budget membership program spas. You're getting a less experienced individual who probably is not giving you the same type of massage that we're offering. I could tell you that they're not giving you the same type of massage that we're offering. So I would say one of the biggest misconceptions in a scenario like that is people think we are the same thing, but we are vastly different from one another. They're great for their market and their type of clientele, and we fit with our market and our type of clientele. I don't think we're competing necessarily for the same kind of clientele, but I do think that sometimes people believe that they're comparing apples to apples in that kind of situation. They're not.

Jeremy Baker: Are there any techniques or treatments that you're offering now that you wish more clients knew about or took better advantage of?

Tiffany: So we just began offering micro-needling, and it's a pretty great service. I think it's something that I'd love our spa clientele to know about mostly because it's a wonderful way to make your skin look great with a minimum commitment of down time. You know, we are definitely ablating the skin, abrading the skin, you're going to look red, but you're going to heal very quickly within less than 24 hours. When it comes to doing medical treatments in our environment, we're trying to stay away from really ablative treatments, have a lot of downtimes. It has just a little bit of down time and a wonderful benefit. It increases collagen production, firmness, laxity in the skin. It's just an excellent treatment for pretty much everyone, male, female, young and old. It does brighten, tighten, and make your skin look a lot better. Who wouldn't want that?

Jeremy Baker: Growing in popularity I might add.

Tiffany: Very much.

Jeremy Baker: Can you describe your ideal client? Regarding what situation they're in, what they're looking to accomplish, how you deliver the results for them.

Tiffany:

Yes. An ideal client for us is typically say 35 to 55 or 60 years old. She or he is looking not to change his or her look, but to embrace their beauty. Our sense of self is kind of involved in how we look. So I would say that women who are trying to come into our environment and look better and feel better about themselves are what we're looking for.

Women who want to relax but also who want to take care of their skin and see some results but are very happy, hopefully, with the way that they look and are not looking to change their looks, just looking to enhance their looks.

Jeremy Baker: O.K, before we end, I want to give you an opportunity to tell the readers and the listeners more about your spa. Anything else you'd like to add?

Tiffany: We have three spas and product stores in those three spas. One is Wellesley and Lexington and one in downtown Boston on Newbury Street. Our Wellesley store has a full-service hair salon. It is extremely popular in this area, and we offer everything from medical treatments, laser hair removal, micro-needling, to your basic spa treatments and massage, nails, manicures, pedicures-all of that good stuff. We're a full-service spa opportunity in New England.

Jeremy Baker: It's been wonderful speaking with you, and it sounds like you have a great spa in Boston. Hopefully, our readers or listeners will be able to take advantage of those services and, once again, it's been wonderful speaking with you.

Tiffany: Thank you so much.

bellasante.com

# DR. YELENA YERETSKY

*Clinique YFT*

Jeremy Baker: My guest today is Dr. Yelena Yeretsky, otherwise known as Dr. Y. She is an internationally recognized specialist in anti-aging, and aesthetic medicine. With many years of experience improving her patient's' appearance, and overall quality of life. A highly intuitive professional, she combines impeccable attention to detail with healing techniques, creates subtle transformations that gracefully rejuvenates the skin, revealing the patient's true character. Of European descent, Dr. Y completed her education at top US Medical institutions and is board certified in internal medicine. For the last 14 years, she has practiced medical and cosmetic dermatology in New York, New Jersey area, building a loyal following of patients. Welcome Dr. Y.

Yelena: Hello Jeremy glad to talk to you here today.

Jeremy Baker: It's great having you. I'm excited to learn more about what you're doing. The first question that I have for you is what inspired you to become a Med Spa owner?

Yelena: Well all my life basically since I was a child, I believed in wellness, and I was obsessed with creating little skin care masks, beauty, anything that has to do with looking good, feeling good, and that type of nature. Growing up in the former Soviet Union we didn't have much to do, so I used natural remedies a lot. And in through years of just travelling through the world, after coming to the United States in 1999 and studying here as you mentioned in my Bio. I collected all this spa information while travelling through the European and American spa.

When I arrived in the United States, the spa concept was not very much developed, and at that time, it was mostly for people with lots of wealth. A majority of people that I met didn't even know anything about just going to sauna, or scrubbing, exfoliating, forget about even medical treatments. But Europeans were always very big about doing facials monthly, about moisturizing the body, about using skin care a lot, even when you were very young. So I always loved that feel of the woman, the young girl as a human being, but I also always knew that I wanted to be a doctor.

So I always knew that I would be in some healing field, and that was never a question for me what kind of profession to choose. So, of course, I became a doctor, and then eventually I end up in aesthetics and anti-aging field. So I graduated in the early 2000 and by that time I already took lots of lots of what we call rotations, in the field of medical aesthetics and anti-aging medicine. I have to say that the field of medical aesthetics is more kind of dramatically together with my career, which is in the last 10, 15 years.

Jeremy Baker: Absolutely.

Yelena: It was nothing and then suddenly became so, so many things. When I started we had Botox, which was still not popular yet even, and we had collagen, bovine, and we had a few lasers and chemical peels, and microdermabrasion machines, just a few stuff. Today we have an incredible amount of so many tools, to make you look beautiful, to make you feel confident and to make you feel great. This side is the medical aesthetics side, and I have taken many, many classes all over the world to try to be the best, and stay on top of everything. I use lots of classes and courses because at that time, as you know very well in residency it was not taught. So you had to learn by yourself, learning all this and I did. Then I started to teach them to others. At the same time, I was part of the dermatology practice, where I practice medical and cosmetic dermatology.

But in the last five years, I said to myself, you know what the field has grown so dramatically, and it's almost whenever new types of patients, meaning people are healthy now. When they come to the physician, it's not a sick individual who needs a prescription; there is more. It's about preventative medicine, and aesthetic medicine is preventative medicine because ultimately you're healthy. You just want to be better, and you want to look better, you want to feel better. So I decided to open something that addresses this particular environment, for somebody like me. Because I'm right now in my early 40's, and ultimately I am the number one customer of myself. And combining kind of two sides of who I am, which is the scientist and all these years of education, and experience, plus me as a woman. Somebody who wants to look my best and feel my best, because that will give me confidence. Also my personal obsession with skincare and the beauty industry, being a socialite and a fashionista living in New York City, and always like travelling and jet-setting.

Then I said to myself you know what, why don't I create a space where people can lay back, individuals who have no time, people who want to look their best in a fast support bottom line pleasant and gorgeous environment. So in 2010, I opened my place, and it's called Clinique YFT. It is a place in West Village which I love, where the hottest and best happens in West Village. Where we created an environment which looks basically like a medical boudoir. It's very sexy and seductive, and it's very clean. It does not look like a medical office at all because there is more to medicine. There's also a future emotional part, of people coming and sharing their needs, and their goals, and their desires.

So the place is very beautiful aesthetically because we're dealing with beauty and aesthetics. We also incorporated not only medical aesthetics services but also traditional wellness kind of old school, the facial features. Being European I still believe the monthly, very good old school looking facials are fabulous. I believe in massage especially medicinal massage, where lots of tensions are, like people sitting in front of a computer, people constantly being on social media. I do believe that taking care of the body is as important, as taking care of the skin. We also do horoscopes for people. So we can discuss the stars and what's happening in the emotional life of human being, which is very, very important. We do tarot cards sometimes. So ultimately we have kind of like a social club of fabulous people, who come and sometimes read poetry, sometimes we have parties. We recently had an event for almost 200 people, with like belly dancers. We're just having fun. Ultimately, my purpose is to bring back the joy of being a woman, the joy of living well, the joy of life itself. We're doing those through by medical background.

So this is what we're doing. My personal attitude towards medical aesthetics is very, very practical. I combine science and luxury. I combine opposite things and bring it to simplicity. The most important thing I believe is consultation. I think today in the 21st century, anybody at any age should, at least, get a consultation, and discuss what the choices are. How they're going to age, what can be done to prevent it, because I do believe the future is in preventative medicine, in every field of medicine. And medical aesthetics being just something that you can see and this is something that's my personal passion and love. But you could look at preventative medicine in the future for any field of medicine. It's the personal desire within our very busy schedule, in such busy life and I do take care of many busy New Yorkers. I have celebrities. I have models. I have mothers. I mean any profession, writers, dancers, artist, so absolutely any profession. Everybody has one thing in common; nobody has time. Not having time is the most important thing. So I will go to give people back the energy, the self-love, the self-love of looking back in the mirror and saying, I look great. I'm exhausted and tired, but you can't see it.

Jeremy Baker: Absolutely.

Yelena: So yes consultation becomes number one priority, because even if people don't do anything, I give them knowledge. I give them knowledge of what's out there because when people read too much of the media, they get confused. And sometimes it's very neatly presented by the media. If you read anything in the magazines, it's like 5 minutes and everything will be solved, and we all know it's not like that.

Jeremy Baker: Yes and like you said before, there are so many more options available now to the consumer. It's easy to get confused on what treatment is best for their situation.

Yelena: This is so true. I know people often come in and say okay I want Botox, and Botox could be choice number 4 once you evaluate their face, and once you look at them. Everybody made need a little Botox here and there, but maybe for this particular person, Botox would not be number one, choice number one. Something that would make a difference in their face, maybe something else would be choice number one. It's what I do as my job, to inform and be like a messenger for these people, to tell them what is most important and how to look your best. That's 1. Number 2 an injectable is not enough because the skin has to grow. Anybody who can be injected every way, if their skin is not glowing, it will not conflate into looking gorgeous.

So it's very important to address skin together with injectables, because it's a very common thing once again of people for example wanting to look good, and then there's skin discolour and sun damage. So even if you want it to be good, it doesn't look beautiful because that's not the purpose. There is no glow in the person. So each person receives a very individual treatment almost like a prescription to their lifestyle. We discuss lifestyle. We discuss options for their face. I always ask people what they like about their face, and what they don't like about their face. It's very important to understand how they always think they are, so you both have realistic expectations of the results. And most importantly, is to know why anybody wants to do it. You should want to do it for yourself, for feeling confident or feeling your best self. But if you're 60 and you want to look 20 that's probably will not be the best approach. It's for you to look your best. Another way I kind of feel right now with young girls, which I call them young kitty cats because when they are together playing around, they sound like a set of kitty cats.

They love to do their lips, so I find it very cute. When I was their age, I was like oh my gosh lip gloss, lip gloss, and then I remember we started getting those plumpers. Like have a little cinnamon or have a little spice or peppermint in the lip gloss 15- 20 years ago and would make them red, and like oh my god I'm plumping my lips. Now they just come and get them injected. So I find it a very cute 21st-century approach, compared to our mothers and grandmothers who were afraid to put lipstick on.

Jeremy Baker: I can see that it's growing. The popularity is growing, acceptance and the age curve is gone down. So regarding the services that you're offering now, what's the most popular service in general?

Yelena: In medical aesthetics I believe that overall Botox would be number 1, and fillers would be number 2. That's what people come for. But I always turn it around in the sense I don't look at it this way. I have a very holistic approach to the face. I deal with the whole face. So when I give my consultation, I discuss the quality of skin care, skin care routine, and then we discuss what I call like a rabbit ear moment, which is how not to look tired. So we end up doing the whole face, and that's why my patients stay with me. They don't leave. I do not do like oh my God, help with my eyes and I just take care of the eye. This is not how I operate because I don't want to be treated like that. So I treat everyone the way I would like to be treated, which is the full face. Usually, it requires a little bit of many things.

It will require a combination of treatments, a little bit of fillers, a little bit of light chemical peel, a little bit of skin care. Right now this coming year 2016, I'm coming out with my line called Dr. Y Secrets which basically, is the line that once again based on everything I mentioned earlier, on years of experience as a woman and years of my experience as a doctor combining science and luxury in a very simple form. I feel it's my purpose in life to try everything that's out there and narrow down on the best. And what works the best, you achieve the best, and what is the most effective under the circumstances for each particular individual. So when I give consultation we both do the whole face, and once again glow of your skin, skin care routine, and my patients end up with absolutely everything. End up having a little Botox, a few fillers, and different types of fillers because it depends on what the issue is. The different parts of the face require different pads. That's why in the media sometimes there are articles like putting one of the fillers above or over another filler, and this is incorrect. Because some fillers are great to put under eyes, other fillers do great in the lips, and other fillers do great in creating a mini face lift.

It also depends on the structure of the patient's face. It depends on how much volume they have. So we have so much that we can do today, which I don't think the approach I see in media which says, I can do this filler, or do that filler gives the right impression on the consumer. 15 years ago, you can be proud that you use certain fillers but today there are more options available. Of course, we all know as physicians how to use them, but the hard part of aesthetics medicine comes from evaluating the face, understanding the beauty of this particular individual, understanding their vision of what they call beauty. And advising them on what would be the best way to achieve that, and then using all those fillers, chemical peels, lasers as toys, toys to play with. For you as an artist to give this person the best possible result, where they'll be natural, beautiful and happy. We have a joke in my office; you never look older than 35. It's our cut off age.

Jeremy Baker: It sounds like you have a very specialized approach and viewpoint on the entire aesthetic process... how you take them from where they are now to where they would like to be.

Yelena: Correct you are so experienced you nailed it down right away. When I meet a new person we discuss what could be done, and they don't have to do it all right away because you need to be ready to do it. It's through science and medicine there's always side effects. So the person can be prepared with their expectation, then we discuss all of that. In the first year of our relationship usually, we dedicate it to getting from where we are, to getting where we want to be. Because a majority of people in New York in West Village, I don't deal with West Village it's just a great place to be. But I deal with many international people, everybody from the United States, so whoever they are. People come in, and they first have to make a decision and it's an emotional process to make that decision. People are afraid to do that. People are afraid how much it cost. People are afraid how they are going to look.

People are afraid whether their husband is going to find out. It's so much of an emotional component, so we take it slowly. Also, majority people can no longer take time off. The old school was I want to stay at home for a week, but who can stay at home for a week, nobody. So majority procedures we have to do it in a way, so the person come back to their lifestyle which is so important, to create a program for people that they can handle and that they can realize. That they can see their lifestyle, it's paramount. It has to be realistic, a realist approach. So then it takes us usually a year to get us where we want to be, and after that we have maintenance. Maintenance is something you just need a little bit The best way is to always do a little bit, than to do everything at once. Some people prefer and that's fine with me.

I will provide it for them as long as they realize that the more material you put in, the more healing time, the more possibility of bruising. When you do a little bit often, nobody knows ever, and it's like this very gradual transformation where even when you're exhausted you never look it.

Jeremy Baker: Makes sense..

Yelena: That's what we do and, of course, we have lots of interesting services. It is Medical Spa but then I have lots of patients, and they get pregnant, then to maintain you can't do anything when you're pregnant. Then they come and see once a month the facials I have. So we have a very special European massage using the hydrating mask. We maintain the pregnancy and while the patient breastfeeds, and then we move back to more aggressive treatments. The key is I think, to know who you are as a business owner, and as a person, and as a doctor, and I think you attract similar people. So for example, I attract men and women who want to look natural, who care about their looks. But at the same time, they are not going to spend time in front of the mirror. They want to know something will work, yes they will do it, but it has to be efficient, effective, practical, and pleasant. We in Clinique YFT we celebrate pleasures of life, so we are immense on using our senses, smelling perfumes, smelling roses. So we incorporate that into our everyday lives.

Jeremy Baker: What about challenges, what's you biggest challenge right now?

Yelena: The biggest challenge I would say is to be on the same page. At the beginning to explain to people everything that can be, and so to have the same expectation. That is very, very challenging because I do it every day of my life, morning to night I basically repeat the same thing, and lots of things to be is very, very kind of like everyday life. But people who come in everything is an issue, and it's a different personality. When a person walks in this whole emotional world coming in, with their life. I think for us to meet so we're on the same page, that could be challenging but usually we solve it. Because to understand for example, that there is the possibility of bruising, the possibility of side effects, that's challenging. Overall I think anytime you're in any business dealing with human beings. It could be challenging.

Jeremy Baker: Sure. How often do you communicate with your client base, via email, social media, text, etc.?

Yelena: Sure. I send four times a year on average I send a newsletter, and my newsletters are gorgeous. Because everything we do, there's patients that even joke that one day they're going to be famous they're so beautiful. It represents everything I do which is the celebration of life and beauty, science, and luxury. Yeah, four times a year, then once a year I throw a very big party which is the kind of my office birthday party, and it's usually in November. We just had ours as I mentioned, with lots of people and performance, jazz singers. We were like Vegas type of party. It's very dramatic, lots of champagnes like boxes and boxes. I think this last party was 53 bottles of champagne.

Jeremy Baker: For 200 people. There were some people leaving, feeling pretty good that night.

Yelena: Yes, yes especially because we had a little burlesque going. I do have not only women; I have lots of men also. I have a very, very eclectic practice. So we have people from every walk of life. And what gives me personally one of the biggest pleasures in life, is when I see all the people of the world come together for this celebrations in the name of beauty. You see Republicans and Democrats together. You see the most conservative or the most liberal. You see gay, straight, you see every walk of life, FBI agent, escort service, and I love it. I find that's what I live for. That's who I am, and that's why I came to live in New York City. Because at the end shows how we are all the same, and we all want to laugh, connect and underneath all of it. What I do through my services, through my life, I'm doing it in the name of beauty into the world.

So that's how I communicate with my patients. So I do not send reminders. I do not do specials.

I communicate on a whole kind of level. Then marketing my business this is my concept. When everything comes out of your face when you wake up in the morning, look in the mirror, and the mirror goes woo, that's the time to come back. I have to tell you, even myself personally because obviously I'm 43. I'm a New Yorker. I used to party a lot. I'm injected; I am a number one customer. Even doing this it's so fun, where you are completely done or injected. You're like I'm fun. I'm so great; I don't need this. I don't need this. Then there is one day you wake up and everything drops. You look in the mirror and go, what happened. How did this happen?

Jeremy Baker: Right. It's not like it wasn't there last week. It's just you didn't notice it and now all of a sudden you're noticing it, right.

Yelena: Exactly. It literally just droops, and you are looking at it like, oh my God what happened? Emergency. People always joke, what kind of Botox emergency can you have. You would be surprised; it is a little like that. One day you were fine, then you are not fine.

Jeremy Baker: When they want their Botox, they want their Botox now.

Yelena: Absolutely. It's not tomorrow, it's not in the month, it's now immediately. Because we celebrate marriages, we celebrate divorces, break ups, and the reaction to this is injectable. It's a very emotional part. That's what doctors have to do on their part, also, step up and give their patients recommendations, not just do business. That is why I think it's so important to evaluate the whole face, because if the person is emotional for whatever reason. Maybe a family member passed away; maybe you break up with a loved one, perhaps you had a fight with your daughter. I don't know something emotional happened. And people come in and like, give it to me, give it to me. I want this change, do it to me. This is where a doctor had to step in and say; okay you know this is not that straightforward. You have to create a plan, where the person is happy, but really beautiful.

Jeremy Baker: Yeah. Speaking of urgency, I'm sure you get some clients that come in that have had treatments at other spas. Are there mistakes that you are seeing them make when they go to other spas and then come to you?

Yelena: Yes definitely. Because I have excellent relationships with my patients, meaning I have splendid retaining patients who when they come to me, they don't leave. I shouldn't say a lot, but I do have patients who need to be corrected, and sometimes it's something simple. And sometimes it requires whatever was done has to come out.

Jeremy Baker: What are some of the mistakes that you see?

Yelena: The mistakes I see are simple ones, with Botox, the eyebrows having too much arch and looking a little scary. So that's very easily correctable. The mistake I see, is people go the wrong places maybe because they found a coupon or something. I think aesthetically; they just don't look good, and the way they were injected it was incorrect for their particular face. Maybe science wise, Clinique wise it was correct but the person doesn't look good, so the art of it is not. I also see sometimes people very much overdone. So along the way sometimes I can correct, sometimes it has to come down. The filler has to be gone. Sorry, this is actually number 1. I would like to say that people are not done as a whole face, going back to the holistic approach. So for example, people come in because they had dark circles under the eye.

They want to have filler there, and they come in, and they have filler in there. They do Botox for example on the forehead, and their chin is drooping, and their cheeks are drooping. So then it's almost obvious that Botox was done, or something was done, and then the rest of the face is drooping. So I don't believe it helps anyone because that's when it becomes so obvious.

Like, hello, you look like you had Botox, and now there's oh I love your Botox, verses hey you know what you look gorgeous. Because ultimately it doesn't matter how old you are. Look at Jane Fonda. I mean look at Jennifer Lopez, and look at Gwen Stephanie. I mean it doesn't matter how old people are. Just look at somebody and say wow, you look great. I think it comes from having a glowing skin, a very glowing skin, no greyness, no darkness, and it comes from not having effects of gravity. Things are not hanging. I think when people concentrate on the current fashion or trend because in medical aesthetics we also have trends. And everybody has those cheeks, and then you still have a chin hanging or something. It doesn't look good. Your face must have some kind of flow, a fluidity to it.

Jeremy Baker: A natural flow right, natural beauty.

Yelena: Yes, A very natural flow that if your forehead gets tightened up, your neck and jaw line should tighten up too. I mean realistically speaking, how much can be done depends on age and skin type, and how much you were taking care of yourself through your lifetime. So yeah when only one piece of the face is done, and everything else is not glowing, is drooping then what's the purpose? Don't do anything.

Jeremy Baker: That makes sense. That's one of the trends that I have noticed in my experience so far. The trend is to enhance the natural beauty, and not just focus on one particular area like you said. Whether it's around the eye, or the forehead. Craft an approach, a long-term approach that makes sense. Instead of just a quick couple of injections here, there and send them on their way.

Yelena: Yes. Also, some of the materials we use today are a long-term investment in the future. Because by fillers, chemical peels. By injecting them they stimulate your collagen production, so this way you benefit from the injection itself, but you also stimulate your collagen which is a long term great result. So once you decide to start enhancing your look, if you stay on top of it for a year I know for sure in the second, especially in the 3rd year you need less, less, and less treatment. You need less and fewer materials because the body doesn't move it completely. So if you always consistently maintain yourself a little bit, it's the same thing as about diet or exercise. If you always eat well, if you always exercise and even a little bit, it's better if you decide to do it for the summer. And go crazy on some binging and craziness. The same thing with medical aesthetics. You always do a little something to maintain your natural freshness. You need less, less and less as you proceed. You never need as much as when you begin.

Jeremy Baker: What service are you offering now, along these lines, that you wish more of your clients took better advantage of?

Yelena: I think my clients end up doing all of them. So I feel like eventually we get there because the way my particular office set up. I manage to persuade them why it's so important. But I do wish that people would never forget their skin care routines. Because people are running after the latest loose ends, and sometimes forget the most basic skin care regimen. Because the fundamental, most basic consistent skin cares, regiments can make miracles, together with very light resurfacing procedures. I wish people paid attention to their skin more.

Jeremy Baker: Can you explain your ideal client , what their current situation is and what they want to accomplish, and then how you help them achieve that goal?

Yelena: My ideal client could be any age, it's a personality trait. It's a character trait of a person who wants to look her best, who wants to know what's available, and wants to learn about the process. So once she or he comes to learn about the world of medical aesthetics, we ultimately become friends, and I tell them about what's available, and the prices. And I love realistic people who can say okay, this is how much I have available, what can be done. And we create a plan of most important, to least important, and they hold their appointment. They trust me, and they always look their best, and that show my whole practice grew by word of mouth because all my patients look the best.

Jeremy Baker: That's wonderful. I appreciate the passion. You can hear the passion in your voice, and your dedication.

Yelena: Thank you.

Jeremy Baker: It's very clear that you enjoy helping your patients, clients achieve their best.

Yelena: I do and definitely a passion of mine, and I can't imagine any other profession. I'm in the right place and the right time.

Jeremy Baker: That's wonderful. Before we go is there anything else that you would like to say, in parting words to those listening and reading the book?

Yelena: I recommend that everybody have a consultation with a medical aesthetic physician, at any age. Just to learn what's out there, and what's possible. When you make that decision later on. What it is that you want to do, you should always speak with the person with whom you're going to do it with.

You should not wait until everything is too late or too scary but just go if it's available. There are so many people doing it, and I think the most important thing is knowledge and self-love. I think in this business that we are in right now, is not a superficial business as so many people think about it. Or the media shows it as a very negative, and very superficial. It is not, and self-love is not superficial. It gives confidence. It gives you that energy and desire to wake up in the morning, and go to that meeting and perform. And to smile, and to have a passionate relationship with your spouse, or your loved one. It gives so much when you look in the mirror, and you love the way you look. So there's nothing superficial about that. I think that it's very important that people should realize that, there are so much available right now, and you go and get a consultation. Nothing needs to be done, just to feel and see what's out there, and it's a beautiful journey, and I welcome everyone to come play with us.

Jeremy Baker: Love it. Those are great parting words, and I think that's a good place to end the interview. Once again it has been a pleasure speaking with you. And for all of those that are listening that would be interested in getting a consultation, the website is cliniqueyft.com. Have a great day.

Yelena: Thank you very much for having me.

cliniqueyft.com

# DR. BOBBY POURZIAEE

*Spa on Rodeo*


Jeremy Baker My guest today is Dr. Bobby Pourziaee. Dr. Pourziaee is the founder of Rodeo Drive Podiatry in Beverly Hills California. He is a Board Certified foot and ankle surgeon and opened the spa with the intention of creating wellness from the ground up. Dr. Pourziaee is a firm believer that healthy feet are the foundation of optimal well-being. To achieve this, Dr. Pourziaee has offered his expertise in tandem with alternative therapies and treatments provided by his staff. The addition of these procedures and the undeniable benefits offered was the inspiration behind the spa. With the Spa on Rodeo Drive, Dr. Pourziaee can now offer the same foundational approach to patients as well as the public. Here the focus starts from the feet and continues up with treatments designed to heal and soothe body and mind. Welcome, Dr. Pourziaee.


Dr. Pourziaee: Hi, hello, thank you.

Jeremy Baker It's great having you on today. I'm particularly interested in hearing about your unique approach to well-being starting with the feet and continuing up, especially as it relates to med spa services. First, give us a general overview of what your approach is as it relates to spa services?

Dr. Pourziaee: Well let me just give a little background. I have been practicing for a little over 14 years in my podiatry practice. Within that practice, we have a heavy focus on biomechanics and also a surgical practice as well. During my time practicing I would dabble in alternative therapies to help patients; anything from neuropathy, circulation issues. But I would try these alternative therapies on patients, and I would see the positive results it would bring. So, therefore, I decided why not take a lot of these therapies I see benefits and just bring it to the public. You don't necessarily have to be a patient of mine, and that's where the spa in Rodeo was born. With every new client that comes in, we take an approach where we start at the feet and work our way up. We do a full evaluation of foot and ankle wellness and from there try to choose an appropriate therapy that would benefit the client.

Jeremy Baker Interesting. Can you describe a podiatry spa service you offer?

Dr. Pourziaee: Yes absolutely, one is our therapeutic foot soak. But every client that comes in either in the podiatry side or the spa, we do a therapeutic foot soak. This foot soaks range in different properties, but essentially they are a detoxifying element to it and a cleansing element as well. We use essential oils and chlorophyll and different things to achieve this.

Dr. Pourziaee: And then from there our treatments kind of focus on different groups. Take for example our massage therapy department. We have treatments that focus on dealing with swelling, so we do a whole cupping series where people come in with chronic edema, and we're able to address this by using cupping therapy. Also reflexology; all our massage therapist trained in reflexology and this is an ongoing art of their education. Some people come in for a lot of different ailments, but the majority come in with usually some type of pain issue, and we're able to address that and monitor it with the reflexology treatments.

Jeremy Baker Ok that's great. What's your most popular service?

Dr. Pourziaee: Definitely on the massage side the cupping. That is very, very popular. People love it, and I think it's just because it works. The people see the benefits from it. Those services are always booked out. From there we have our revision skin treatments. We use a line of skin care products and treatments that will change the issues. So with relation to lower extremities, people will have capillaries or scars or anything like that. We will go in and change that up to a level. Some patients will come in and say they've gone to different plastic surgeons and dermatologists, and they can't treat this. They'll come in and after a series of treatments; we'll see some real changes as well.

Jeremy Baker. So the cupping, I know that is used in acupuncture, is it the same basic concept when you use it on the feet.

Dr. Pourziaee: The cupping is essentially the same type of procedure. Obviously, there is a variation of size of cups and how you create the suction, but the overall philosophy is the same.

Jeremy Baker Ok interesting. What would you say makes your spa unique? Obviously, your approach to spa services focusing on the feet is unique. Is there anything else that would make you stand out?

Dr. Pourziaee: I would say that it is our personalized and customized treatments that we give. So when somebody comes in, a lot of ways we assess them is like a doctor's office because that's what I do first. So we will do a complete assessment of them and see what different things they would benefit from. Also, it's the follow through and the monitoring of all of our services. We just don't say "oh just come in once per week" and don't do any follow-up. We are touching base with our clients and making sure they're achieving their goals, whether it's relief from pain or whether it's more beautiful skin, whatever the goals are of the client we are monitoring it.

Jeremy Baker That's critical. So you would say that you are getting many of your patients as regular clients by reaching out and communicating with them on a regular basis?

Dr. Pourziaee: Absolutely. And that's a big part of what I do with the spa part of it involves just making sure that again, whether you are technically a patient or just a spa client, I treat it all the same way. So it is that personalized service, that high-level service what we know everybody is there for and we do our best to help them achieve that.

Jeremy Baker Which is obviously one of the reasons why you are successful in what you are doing. Is there anything else you can attribute your success to?

Dr. Pourziaee: I would say it is my team. My team is incredibly talented. They are very well experienced. It is finding that right therapist technician and creating a group of therapists that communicate with each other and that have the client's well-being as their priority.

Jeremy Baker What is your biggest challenge right now?

Dr. Pourziaee: The biggest challenge right now. The thing is, a lot of times people will come in with the newest fad. So whether it is the new laser, that's out, whether it's something new and all the other doctors are doing it. It's about us understanding what this new thing is but also educating the client that maybe you don't necessarily need this. Maybe the things that we already do achieve that and you're better off doing that. So it's that communicating with the newest and greatest thing.

Jeremy Baker: And that brings me to my next question; what are the mistakes that you commonly see some of your clients make when they are going to other Spas for other spa services and then come to see you?

Dr. Pourziaee: The mistake that I see is when things are overdone. Let's take skin treatments: one peel will achieve this but if I go every week or if I go three times a week I'm going to get a. Some places will just do it, rather than say no, this is not what you need let's space this out. So people get excited, and it's about monitoring and taming it and giving them a long term goal. So some people are disappointed and go to other places, and you just understand why that happened. A lot of times they just over do it.

Jeremy Baker: So we talked about the communication between the clients, and it sounds like you do a great job with that. How often do you communicate with them and how do you communicate with them? For instance social media, email, text et cetera.

Dr. Pourziaee: Really all of the above. The most important are the personal one on one. As they come in, they know. Each visit, whether it's me or my Director of Operations, we are at the higher level; they get a conversation with us. And then also, every day with the client list, we review as a group who is there and making sure we address any special needs for that day and making sure everybody is on a goal. That's the most important. From there we communicate on social media. We have a large media presence. So anything new, any specials, we try to blast it through social media. Also communication through phone calls and text messages and emails. We do all of that. When somebody becomes a client, we find out their preference in communication. I know myself, I love text messages, and emails take me a while to respond to. That's just my preferred way. So we find out what the clients preferred way is, and we just make it. We don't want to be a burden on them. We want to add to their life.

Jeremy Baker Right it's interesting for you to talk about texts like that because I wholeheartedly agree with you. Email is great you should continue to use it, but the reality of it is, open rates are pretty low on emails and texts always get opened and read, so you just have to be careful about making sure that they understand why they are getting the text from you. And as long as they know who you are and expect a text from you then it's great. It's a wonderful way to communicate with clients.

Dr. Pourziaee: Absolutely.

Jeremy Baker: What are the procedures and services that you offer that you wish more clients knew about or took better advantage of?

Dr. Pourziaee: That we offer? Let me see. We have a new type of procedure that we just introduced, and it's not even on our menu yet. But it is a massage therapy using bamboo sticks, so this is something that we are excited about, and we want everyone to know about. We just literally started it two weeks ago. That's an exciting one. Going back to wellness from the ground up, we offer obviously manicures and pedicures and being a foot doctor I know a special amount of information about proper pedicure protocols. That's something that especially men don't think of their feet as being that important. They think "oh I'm not going to get a pedicure, it's really for women. It's more of a Frou-Frou thing". Where in fact there are medical benefits to getting a proper pedicure. We've seen people come in who have never gotten pedicures before. And the way we do it it's a sterile medical pedicure that's the best way to describe it. But all our nail technicians are trained under me to look for signs of infection, anything that can cause problems. We've even had people that didn't know they had diabetes and just off the cuff say "oh I don't have that much feeling in my toes" and then we can address that specifically and work on them properly that's referring to the medical part of the business. But the level of services that we offer for the manicures and pedicures, the high level, I wish more people would get involved with that because it's very important.

Jeremy Baker: It sounds like what you are offering here is an expanded service for a pedicure, different from what they would get at a nail salon place.

Dr. Pourziaee: Correct...

Jeremy Baker: Regarding your clientele, can you just briefly describe what you would consider your ideal client to be? What their situation is, what they're looking to accomplish and how you accomplish that? Obviously, every patient is unique, but a general overview.

Dr. Pourziaee: Yeah I mean our ideal clientele if we are talking about somebody that hasn't been in yet, so it's somebody who's reached a point in their life where they are having a little bit more pain. They're starting to have some medical issues. So they have a renewed interest in their health. The best thing for them to do is to come in and let us be a springboard to see what that is. So it's something we can help with. Maybe it involves more comprehensive services that we don't offer. But that person is usually in their 40's and 50's, starting to kind of move up in life and they want to walk better, they want to look better, they want to feel better, and usually the spa is the perfect place for that person to come in and just explore those things.

Jeremy Baker: Before we go why don't you tell us how to find you? Your website is rodeodrivepodiatry.com, is that correct?

Dr. Pourziaee: Correct. So the practice is rodeodrivepodiatry. com, and the Spa website is spaonrodeo.com, and we are also on Instagram and Facebook and Twitter.

Jeremy Baker: Great. It sounds like you are the man to see when it comes to these services that are related to the feet.

Dr. Pourziaee: Absolutely.

Jeremy Baker Anything else you would like us to know before we go? It's been wonderful and very informative speaking with you,

Dr. Pourziaee: Yeah absolutely. I just encourage everybody to look us up on our website and to reach out and to give us a try.

Jeremy Baker Great thanks again and have a wonderful day.

# DR. ARLENE NOODLEMAN

*Age Defying Dermatology*

Jeremy: My guest today is Dr. Arlene Noodleman. Arlene is CEO and medical director of the "Healthstyle Integrative Medicine Center". She's also CEO of Silicon Valley's Age Defying Dermatology and co-creator of Revercel clinical skin care products and nutritional supplements.

Dr. Noodleman holds BA and MD degrees from the University of Minnesota and received her Master's in Public Health (MPH) degree from the University of California-Berkeley. She is board certified in preventive medicine and fellowship-trained at the University of Arizona Center for integrative Medicine under the direction of Dr. Andrew Weil.

Dr. Noodleman works with her patients to prevent chronic disease, delay the inevitable age related decline in health for as long as possible and helps people compress the morbidity of aging for greater vitality and longevity.

Welcome Dr. Noodleman; it's an honor to have you on today.

Dr. Noodleman: Thank you, it's a pleasure to be here.

Jeremy: What was your inspiration for opening Age Defying Dermatology?

Dr. Noodleman: "Age Defying Dermatology" is our dermatology medical center, which is directed by my husband, Dr. Rick Noodleman, Stanford, Harvard and Duke trained, board certified dermatologist. Healthstyle Integrative Medicine is a separate division of Age Defying Dermatology where we practice integrative medicine and preventive medicine, my inspiration and my passion.

I'm board certified in preventive medicine and have always been passionate about health promotion and disease prevention. In a complementary way, my husband's interest is in the 'outer envelope' of the body, which is the skin, and how it reflects what's going inside. Together, the two aspects of what we do in our medical center work really well together.

Jeremy: Okay great, so is the Age Defying Dermatology the aesthetic side of the business?

Dr. Noodleman: Yes. We provide our patients with a broad spectrum of medical and cosmetic dermatology services including work with lasers, radiofrequency (RF), and minimally invasive cosmetic surgery, all done under local (not general or spinal) anesthesia.

We are located in Silicon Valley so we see a lot of very busy people, professionals and people who want to look better incrementally. We offer a "not-so-extreme-make over" and so we offer a vast array of dermatology services, from skin cancer surgery, also called Mohs surgery, to aesthetic resurfacing of the skin. The nice thing about skin resurfacing is that skin that looks better is actually healthier skin. And we always recommend our patients go on a home skin care regimen, which is so important. My husband and I co-created the Revercel product line. Some people think it's spelled "reversal", but we spell it "Revercel" because our products reverse the signs of aging at the cellular level. Our website www.revercel.com offers these products for everyone. Because home care is really the foundation. It's great to make an investment in your skin but, without a home care regimen, the results can't be maintained or augmented over time.

In addition, Age Defying Dermatology also has a world-class Medi-Spa with aesthetician services including Silkpeel which your listeners are probably familiar with. This is a crystal-less microdermabrasion treatment with a dermal infusion of medically active ingredients such as hyaluronic acid, skin lighteners and anti-acne solutions. In several treatments we get the same results we achieved as years ago with chemical peels. So now we do fewer and fewer chemical peels and more and more Silkpeels. We also offer our patient-clients therapeutic facials and the Refinity peel.

At Healthstyle, we practice integrative medicine, a healing-oriented medicine that takes account of the whole person (body, mind, and spirit), including all aspects of lifestyle. It emphasizes the therapeutic relationship and makes use of all appropriate therapies, both conventional and alternative. It's really 'lifestyle medicine'. We help our patients increase their 'healthspans' as well as their lifespans. Instead of focusing on disease management, we focus on health promotion and the changes people can make to increase their quality of life and vitality. So that Healthstyle. A long answer to your question!

Jeremy: Great.

Dr. Noodleman: Healthstyle practitioners offer integrative medicine consultations, acupuncture, naturopathic medicine, energy work such as healing touch, stress reduction programs, nutritional counseling, and exercise prescriptions. Taken together, we look from the inside-out and from the outside-in so our patients can 'Look and Live Well'. We believe that's what people are looking for.

Jeremy: You sound very passionate about what you do.

Dr. Noodleman: I am!

Jeremy: What you like most about it?

Dr. Noodleman What I like most about what I do is seeing the lasting changes we make in people's lives. Behavioral change is very different from getting a prescription or having a procedure. While I believe in Western medicine, my passion is helping people actively make changes in how they live their lives. Usually, these kinds of changes are incremental. People need to understand that. The journey never ends; change never ends. So when our patients can really see and experience the changes in their lives, that's what I enjoy the most.

Jeremy: What are some of the most popular treatments that you're offering now? On the aesthetic side?

Dr. Noodleman: On the aesthetic side, in addition to home skin care and helping people understand how to maintain their results, the most popular treatments we're offering now use radiofrequency,. Because the trend is how can we make changes in the quality of the skin. We think of aging in terms of as "the three D's": deterioration (usually from sun damage), descent (sagging from gravity) and deflation (changing from a "grape to a raisin"!). RF significantly helps to reduce descent and deflation. There's no downtime because it works from underneath the skin to stimulate cells to produce their own collagen. And because loss of collagen is a hallmark of aging; increasing it is key to having a more youthful look.

And as we age, shrink and shrivel a little bit. RF tightens and plumps the skin in a way that looks very natural. This is probably our biggest trend because there's no downtime, it's "easy in, easy out", and people love their results..

Jeremy: What's that service called?

Dr. Noodleman: It's RF and there are different medical devices on the market. We use a platform. called "Thermi". There are have different types of "Thermi": ThermiSculpt, "ThermiRase, and ThermiLift. RF energy is delivered with a handpiece, much like an aesthetician would use for microdermabrasion, but in this case the wand delivers RF to the skin's deeper layers..

Jeremy: That's interesting. So this show and this book is all about Med-Spa success. and I can see that you are successful. What would you attribute your success to?

Dr. Noodleman I think that the number one the way I measure success is by the results our patients have. We've been in Silicon Valley for over 30 years and we've treated tens of thousands of patients and clients. The reason for this success is because we deliver the results people want and we strive to exceed their expectations. Our patient-clients know this and trust us. We build lifelong relationships with them. People know what they can expect and we deliver. We keep our promises. We have high customer loyalty and repeat business over decades. That's what we attribute our success to. And having the amazing, qualified staff is key.

Jeremy: What would you say your biggest challenge is now?

Dr. Noodleman: There's always competition and we need to help the potential patient-customer see what our value proposition is and how we differentiate ourselves. There is a lot of "noise" in a cluttered marketplace, a lot of "doc in the boxes". Sometimes people find the convenience of having a service in the mall appealing. Sometimes people think of what we do as only about price. We are not a discount operation (although we do offer promotions from time to time). Many of these places use older, outdated technology, too. They may be using a first generation radio frequency device; there's greater discomfort with those earlier devices such as Ulthera, and the results are not as good. However, the consumer may not understand that there's a difference. .

I think we do a pretty good job of communicating to the public but there's so much out there that sometimes people get confused and think: "OK, I can do it more cheaply if I go to this other place. It sounds similar to what Age Defying Dermatology has, but It's cheaper. I can save some money by going there.".

So we have to overcome that way of thinking with a value proposition that includes state-of-the-art technology, a staff of highly trained professionals, and the continuity of care encompassing all issues relating to healthy skin and youthful body contour. A smaller clinic or medi-spa simply can't do what we can do. Copycats who try to make it look as if they do what we do, simply can't. And once people understand that, we win.

Jeremy: Makes sense. Along that line, "educating your client base or your future client base", how often do you communicate with them via communication forms? social media, email, text etc.?

Dr. Noodleman: We use social media, Facebook. We send out regular e-blasts and monthly e-newsletters. But we have to be careful not to over saturate the customer and to always provide rich content, not just a promotion or event..

Because we have so many services and have a lot of seminars and events, we have to be careful not to inundate people's Inboxes. So we're careful. We blog of course and we really want them to be educational so people derive value from them. Lots of relevant content is also good for search engine optimization (SEO) when people search for certain terms on the web. There is a lot of a sophistication and complexity in doing this right. It's easy to just post and blog and tweet, but after a while people begin to ask: is this really giving me value? is this information I can use in my life?

And so we're mindful as we navigate this rapidly changing area.

Jeremy: Clients don't wanna feel like they're constantly getting a sales pitch on every piece of information that comes out.

Dr. Noodleman: That's right. It's also important that prospective clients have a sense of comfort and ease with your organization and don't feel like the only goal is a transaction. We want to build long term relationships and have our referrals come from happy patients and clients. That's what's important. We are not interested in putting things on sale so the focus is just about price. Yes, we of course have occasional discounts and promotions but our focus is being a place where people know that we have their best interest at heart.

Jeremy: That's great. It's good to know. You talked about, some of the competition in the area, the lower price competition. "Doc in a Box", in malls, etc. but when you see clients that come to you and are coming to your med-spa, what type of the mistakes are you seeing them making? When they are coming from other spas?

Dr. Noodleman: I think again, a lot of it is the focus on price and the misconception that these services are a commodity as opposed to a treatment that also depends on the skill and experience of the practitioner or clinical aesthetician. Sometimes people ask themselves, "how little can I pay for this?" We say to our patients and clients that we may not be the most inexpensive clinic or medi-spa that you have seen, but usually we're also not the highest either. It's about more than money.

Our fees are fair and affordable for the vast majority of people that come to us for minimally invasive surgery, for example. We also offer zero interest financing through Care Credit. This is a big help to people. But again, at the end of the day, they have to understand our value proposition: the continuity where they will see the same providers over time, that we don't have the kind of turnover where there's a different aesthetician every time they come in or a different dermatologist. We want our clients to feel like we're a family, from the moment that they enter our doors. We encourage them to bring their spouse or significant other with them or their teenagers with acne or aging in-laws. We have something to offer all of them.

So I think again, people who look for a deal, who think " I want a quick fix in one treatment". Sometimes that's OK. However, so much of what we do is through incremental change. We want their friends to notice that they look better, but never "done". That's why radiofrequency or our lasers are so popular. And we want each person to follow-up with an aesthetician for maintenance too. So much of our approach is having a series of treatment followed by ongoing maintenance.

This is just what we do on the Medi-Spa side with facials and Silkpeels: people need maintenance treatments to keep and augment their results. They need home skin care, too. Once a patient becomes educated and "gets it", once the light bulb goes off, they're hooked. They're customers for life.

Jeremy: Excellent What service or aesthetic treatment are you offering now that you wish more clients knew about or took better advantage of?

Dr. Noodleman: We do a good job in customizing what each person needs. We want every patient-client to see one of our Patient Care Coordinators (PCCs). These are our liaisons. I don't know what other job titles would be appropriate. A coach perhaps. A consultation with a PCC is complimentary; there's no charge. The PCC is at the heart of the patient-client relationship; s/he understands what is bothering them, what their goals are. And we then create an individualized treatment program for them.

Of course, there's always new technology such as radio frequency. Other technologies have been around much longer and can be as valuable as ever. Again, the "secret sauce" for us is creating a program and helping people understand that we're all about developing a long term relationship based on trust. There's a near term need perhaps, such as a wedding you want to look great for. But then there are always concerns about the Three D's that need to get fully addressed over time.

I guess my answer is we don't just focus on one thing, one "flavor of the month". It's many flavors -- over time: home care, light therapy, RF, laser resurfacing, liposuction, a neck lift or eyelid rejuvenation. Because we have so many offerings, we create that customized program and follow-up with each person over time.

Each one of us continues to get older and, as we age, there's an ongoing need to visit us.

Jeremy: Great. So how would you describe your ideal client?

Dr. Noodleman: Our ideal client is a person who is ready for change. Who realizes that what they've been doing isn't working, be it their skin or for their body. It's a person who realizes that they don't like the changes they see in the mirror or their lifestyle. Many patients tell us they've looked in the mirror and the person they see no longer looks like who they think they are. And so they're ready to make a change. Our ideal client has heard great things about us from friends or family. They're already "sold" because and they know that they've come to a place where they'll get the help they need because we have the staff and the "toolbox" to help them. So that's the ideal client, that someone with that mindset

Jeremy: Great! Well we are about out of time. But before we end the interview, I wanna give you an opportunity to let our readers and listeners know anything else you'd like us to know about Age Defying Dermatology or your medical practice.

Dr. Noodleman: Sure. I'd like your readers and listeners to know that we're here to help. We'll listen to your needs and create a customized, results-driven plan for you. We located are in the San Jose area in the heart of Silicon Valley. So please come and see us.

If you're outside of our area check out our websites: www.revercel. com and that's "R E V E R C E L", for the highest quality skincare.

Jeremy: Excellent! And I should add for everyone on the call here, reading this, the website is Agedefy.com

Dr. Noodleman: Yes, in addition to Agedefy.com and Revercel.com, visit our integrative health website www. healthstylecenter.com..

Jeremy: Okay! Great! Well Dr. Noodleman once again it's been wonderful speaking with you and learning about your approach to beautiful skin and anti-aging and I hope you have a wonderful day.

Dr. Noodleman : Thank you for having me.

# BONUS INTERVIEW!

## HOLLY PORTER

*The Image Designers*

Jeremy: My guest today is Holly Porter. Holly is the founder of The Image Designers, and she is not only an image consultant, but she is also an experienced cosmetologist, master aesthetician, make-up artist and instructor educator. (Holly you now have your coaching certification). With over 30 years in the beauty industry, Holly has proven she knows what it takes to make clients look good, on and off the stage. With her interior design background, she brings in color with design line, and personality profiling for the perfect balance, so that anyone can shine their truth. She has been a salon spa owner and manager for over 17 years. Holly understands the ins and outs of the business and working with people. Her hobbies include making people shine with total makeovers, and she loves to see the results of her creations. Raising eight children who are now adults, she currently takes her talent on the road and is one of the few image consultants, who will come to the client. Holly is a speaker and has helped author articles in her industry, who continues to update and educate herself with current trends in the field of beauty. Welcome, Holly.

Holly: Hi how are you?

Jeremy: I'm well. It's great to have you. I'm excited to learn about your perspective in this industry.

Holly: Well thank you. I thank you for having me. It's an honor.

Jeremy: Great. So I'm curious how you got started as an image consultant.

Holly: Well I think it's in my makeup, being raised by an interior designer. I was raised with that background. My mom was also a cosmetologist, and so I had that. I just always loved playing in hair, so that's where I started. Then a few years after that is when I got my aesthetics license because I liked to make up as well. So that's been all of my life.

I just always loved the whole experience, from start to finish on people. You can do a lot for somebody's image in a few hours. So that's all.

Jeremy: Okay. Can you tell us a little bit about what your background is in the beauty industry?

Holly: Yes. I went to beauty school right out of high school. I got a scholarship through a beauty pageant that I was in, so I came back and used that to enter the field like literally right out of high school. I have always done hair and makeup. In addition, I was raised by a father that was in the construction business, and I've always had a husband who's been in the construction industry, so I've always worked in that arena as well. So it just seems like I had my hands in business operations, but I always was in hair always. I hate to age myself, but it's been over 30 years now that I have worked in this industry.

Jeremy: So can you talk to us a little bit about challenges that you've had to overcome in your business?

Holly: I think my biggest problem is the image, and now that's what I specialize in. I was bullied as a child, and I had two best friends and went home daily crying because no three girls can hang out together- 3 isn't a good combination. I always kind of felt like the odd little one out, the ugly duckling. I think the challenge is circled 'am I good enough, smart enough, pretty enough, playful enough, fun enough'? It's huge just knowing that you are good enough, living your truth when you are correct in the colors that you wear, and you feel good about yourself. So I think those have been the biggest challenges, is just fighting for my image and my beauty, to realize that what matters is what I think matters.

Jeremy: Is that something that you help your clients with? Can your image consulting clients overcome the challenges and issues with their professional image, their self-image?

Holly: Yes. I can help clients. I am a certified coach for personal and professional transformation. I am also a certified hypnotist. Hypnosis is a tool that can benefit people who are working on their inner self; it helps the light shine through them. I think a lot of people have the wrong idea of what hypnosis is and you can dig deep. Clients can open up possibilities once they discover what's in the way. Sometimes there's an incident in somebody's life, maybe just someone said the wrong thing at the wrong time, and those words have affected their image of their entire life. Sometimes just little tweaks in the mind can help us change our perceptions of how we look, and how we feel. The deal is this: your image on the outside actually begins on the inside. Have you ever met somebody who at first appears to be a beautiful person on the outside, but they're just plain ugly inside? These people do not glow? The goal is to help each customer radiate, inside out. That's beauty.

Jeremy: Absolutely. The beauty I've always known and wholeheartedly believed radiates from the inside out.

Holly: Absolutely. When people are going and working on their personal development, an image is a big part of your personal development. If you're doing personal work and you're beautiful inside, it's going to radiate outside. What I help do is work with the right color, so that when that person walks into a room, everyone in the room turns and does a double take – something about that person just shines. They're very charismatic, and everybody just looks and goes 'I want to know that person because they glow, they radiate'. You don't notice the detail of their clothes when they walk in, and you notice them as a whole radiant person. That is what I do for people. That is my gift.

Jeremy: So why don't you describe an ideal client for you, and what you do for them?

Holly: Well I want an ideal client to know that they matter. A few changes and I can have them be that person that walks into the room and gets noticed. So if they are wearing the true colors they radiate. Maybe they are an executive, maybe they are even a celebrity, a speaker, an author and they just need to get that extra polish. A lot of people I have interviewed are entrepreneurs starting up new businesses. I have also interviewed quite a few successful entrepreneurs. Whether new or seasoned, they said for a fact that they would not be so successful if they had not hired somebody to work with them with their colors and design image. It's what to wear and how to wear it. My ideal clients would be the types of people who are open to risk and who want to move ahead. They want more in life. I can help anyone wake up to a whole new world of possibilities, give them a new makeover. Remember. I do go to the client, and I spend 2 full days with them, making these changes. My ideal clients are those people who want to design a successful image that allows them to radiate as they enter a room.

Jeremy: It seems by how you're describing it; you work a lot with really helping their self-confidence.

Holly: Yes. I actually start with a personality profile, and I use several different ones. Depending on who they are and how they test on the first profile I may give them a more in-depth profile assessment. Before I even get to them, I give them a personality profile test and I do a color analyzing based on pictures that they send me. Did you know that 80% of your personality is in your eyes? Most people don't know that. So I really, really do some research before I even go to work with the client. I want a customized understanding of the person I am working with, and knowing what general area we're going to be working in. There are so many personality tests and assessment tools out there and with so much information that is sometimes overwhelming. My answer is to combine features of the profiles. I've never found one that's totally complete or perfect, even though I enjoy and can resonate with everything it says. By combine, I mean that I take a little bit from here and a little bit from there, and I just create as complete a profile as possible. I always give the profile name and credit the publisher when I'm working with people because I don't need to create my own. All this is done before I arrive to work onsite with the customer. Then when I get to them, I can begin The Image Design – work with the colors that work with the skin tone. It's harder to do that online because of lighting and context.

Jeremy: Why don't you just go over specifically what you offer? Just kind of take us through where you start, and then where they end up to where they are on the stage full of confidence and looking great.

Holly: I offer clients many packages. My favorite package is the VIP 2-day on-site consultation. It's my favorite because my entire two days are focused on this one client. It is such a rewarding experience. Before I show up, I interview the customer so that I have an understanding of their goals. Then they send me some pictures and complete the personality profile overview. We schedule my 2 day visit and then I fly to work with them. These 2 days are devoted to a package of services. We have the personality profile, the makeover, the color analysis, and we work on what to wear and how to wear it. The personality profile results help us build that confident radiant person within. The makeover, the hairstyling according to movement, the clothes lines that incorporate the colors and design for this person will all reflect that radiant confident person. We take photos and create a book so that the client can continue to use these tools long after I have gone. When I walk out the door, there are 5-10 outfits they have ready to go. They know they're going to turn heads. Now that they understand the colors that are best suited for them, the client can shop with success. It's easier because they know which colors are going to shine on you with your eyes. It is such a rewarding experience.

'Dreams by Design' is a Business Breakthrough Experience. I offer this 12-week workshop both live and online. Clients discover how to live life on their terms, make every day their A Game, and how to live with consistent action. As a certified coach and instructor/educator, I am excited to offer this new business breakthrough opportunity. The program comes with tickets to semi- events that are found on my website: www.the imagedesigners.com.

'Million Dollar Image Consultation' is a shorter program than the VIP program. However, it includes the building blocks that are offered in the VIP program. This includes a personality profile, a personalized color pallet, a discussion of what to wear and how to wear it, and offers an energy flow analysis. The consultation is customized to the client, but does not include any on-site visit.

'Attracting Abundance Imagery Session' is now available as a live seminar or through the purchase of a CD. This is the gift that keeps on giving because it helps those who have the image design piece down, work on their dream life for wealth and relaxation. The benefits are totally amazing. I think anyone who is going through transformation will be over-the-moon with the incredible results from this program.

Those clients who want a piece of this program and a portion of that program are welcome to contact me. We can work out a customized package that will meet their needs. (See contact information at the end of article).

Jeremy: Interesting.

Holly: As you can see the business offerings are evolving. This gives a good overview.

Jeremy: Yeah that's interesting. I'm also curious, how do you get your clients now?

Holly: Clients come from workshops, corporate events, seminar offerings, and speaking engagements. Clients also come from local business acquaintances that learn of offerings by word of mouth. I also offer tickets for one and two-day events to businesses in the community. Some clients are from young entrepreneurs in the region, or as referrals from the advanced technology programs at our local colleges. As I am on my journey, I have found that networking is also a valuable resource for The Image Designers to find clients. Research has shown us that strangers evaluate us on everything from intelligence to trustworthiness in the first 7 seconds of seeing us.

(From Business Insider 02.10.2013)

Jeremy: Right. So you do this individually direct to the consumer. But then do you also work with spas and salons to offer these programs?

Holly: Yes, that's absolutely right. Spas and Salons have a keen awareness of the need for a business like 'The Image Designers'. If we can spread the word, and extend the service, we will be servicing our network of clients in the community. I am working on a starter kit so that other salon operators can take my program and run with it. I can see that this is something that will be great to offer their clients. If I came to their town and in their spa, and did a VIP visit for their client, that is easy. The salon operator would still be doing their hair, their makeup, nails etc... I'm not stepping on any toes like that because I don't want to take that business away from salon or spa owners. What I offer is 2 days. I'm in and I'm out. I created a maintenance program as well. I had people randomly send me text when they're out shopping. What do you think of this outfit? Is it time to change seasons? This maintenance part of the program may lead to a post VIP connection such as a call once a month for a closet tweak, or a shopping tweak, or whatever they need.

Jeremy: Yeah I know I think that's interesting. That's all the questions that I have for now. But before we go why don't you take this opportunity, if there's anything else that you'd like to explain to the listeners or readers, about you and what you do. Take the opportunity to let us know.

Holly: Okay thank you. Here's my contact information. If you want to find out more information, again I'm Holly Porter, and it's The Image Designers: www.theimagedesigners.com

My website has the most current information on my programs, tickets to events, and workshop schedules. We look forward to hearing from you; we are just a click away.

Jeremy: That's entirely correct and like you said it's a small world. So anyone out there that's interested in contacting Holly, feel free to do so. She does offer those consultations. Holly it's been great speaking with you and learning more about what you do.

Holly: Thank you so much, Jeremy, I appreciate it.

Made in the USA
San Bernardino, CA
07 August 2019